The Coach–Approach Leader
Questions, Not Answers, Make Great Leaders

Steve Gladis, Ph.D.

HRD Press, Inc. • Amherst • Massachusetts

Published by: HRD Press, Inc.
                 22 Amherst Road
                 Amherst, MA 01002
                 413-253-3488
                 800-822-2801 (U.S. and Canada)
                 413-253-3490 (fax)
                 www.hrdpress.com

ISBN 978-1-61014-251-9

Editorial services by Joanne Lozar Glenn and Donna Gladis
Production services by Jean Miller
Cover design by Eileen Klockars

Disclaimer

Dedication

This book is dedicated to my newest grandson, Isaiah Dove, who is not only the cutest little guy of his age, but also whose take-it-all-in, unflappable personality style has him already on the coach-approach path.

Contents

Introduction: The Coach-Approach and The Leadership Fable

This book was written for leaders who must make decisions, develop people, and produce a product or a service for either a for-profit or nonprofit organization. As one who has led people in government, private industry, the military, and nonprofits, I'm well aware of what it takes—often under extreme conditions—to get tough things done, i.e., grow people, produce revenues, and pay bills.

Having also been a professor of leadership and communication for many years in both academic and corporate venues, I can boldly say that the key principles in this book—*The Coach-Approach Leader*—are the best that I know at producing leadership results and developing new leaders for tomorrow. But I'll let you judge that claim and hope you'll send me your direct feedback. You'll find my contact information at the end of the book.

The book is divided into two parts:

Part I explains the coach-approach to leadership. It's written like an article you might read in the *Harvard Business Review*, *Training and Development*, or a similar management journal. However, I explain the approach as if you were sitting in one of my classes, which I hope you will find comprehensible, entertaining, and valuable.

Part II tells a story—a leadership fable. It's a fictionalized case study about how this technique works in "real life." I've been teaching the coach-approach technique for years, especially to my corporate and government clients. This story is a fable, a collage of circumstances and experiences that are close to life, but the story and the characters are entirely fictional to better demonstrate the processes. It's worth noting that the research on storytelling as an instructional and motivational tool is compelling. Storytelling aids memory, helps people make sense of complex information, and facilitates their passing along the story and its teachings to others.

Further, the book and the story are written so that everyone in a company—from the stockroom to the boardroom—can read it, providing a common language within the company about the most important, organizational sustaining product of all: Leadership.

Part I
The Coach-Approach Leader

There's a line outside your door. Your direct reports wait to get time on your schedule to talk about a burning issue or problem they're facing. At the end of the day, you're exhausted—spent from dispensing so much advice. The next day, it starts all over again—people want access to your answers.

In fact, since grade school, we've all been primed to have the right answer; I call it the "answer-person syndrome." We get gold stars, good grades, and even promotions at work, all based on having the right answer. Here's the problem: You really can't know all you need to know in order to make accurate decisions on the many and diverse areas that come at you as you ascend the leadership ladder. Eventually, every leader finds this out, and some will seek an executive coach to help them navigate these choppy waters.

While not new, leadership coaching still remains vague, even mysterious. It's surrounded by a host of misconceptions, the most significant of which is that coaches will give clients advice to make them more effective and their companies more profitable. In fact, considering how many clients successful coaches have and how varied their clients' professions (medicine, law, finance, technology, and more), it would be impossible for any one coach to know all those fields well enough to offer even fair advice. On the other hand, successful professional coaches do know *the process* that is capable of moving clients toward sustainable success—regardless of their field.

In short, good coaches own the coaching process, and their clients own the content. This is THE critical distinction between the two roles in the coach-client relationship and what separates coaching from consulting.

As important as it is for leaders to get coaching when they need it, it's just as important for leaders to coach their direct reports when those people come to them with burning issues or problems.

Why? Three reasons:

1. Coaching provides a reliable process, a checklist to help you sift through issues or problems, on any topic or level of complexity.

2. Coaching slows down thinking! Because it is a question-based method, coaching makes us slow down and become both mindful and deliberative, especially when addressing critical questions.

3. Coaching makes your job easier—you never have to bear the pressure of having all the answers. Just master the process, and your questions will help others answer their own questions. Also, it's an easy process to learn!

So, as a value proposition, how does that sound—coaching has high impact on you and it's easy to learn? To add to the value proposition is a kind of "money-back" guarantee: If you do coaching well, the process works—period.

Now let's take a look at the heart of the matter:

- The key elements of the coaching process.

- How to use the coach-approach process with direct reports, peers, bosses, even prospective clients.

- How to use the coach-approach process with teams.

The Key Elements of the Coach-Approach Process

Many people learned basic skills of leadership from the military, either directly or indirectly. The command-and-control model of leadership has been woven into the history of our country and the fabric of modern-day leadership. Authority, one of six key elements of influence, has been documented as a powerful influencer by Robert Cialdini. Authority influences us because no one can know everything. We don't have the time to grab a mechanical or technical certification or a degree in dentistry or medicine in our spare time. So, we consult "specialists" who have the knowledge or expertise we lack. For example, when your car is not working, you take it to your mechanic. When your tooth aches, you go to your dentist. You go to your doctor and expect that she can handle your illness. She has authority in the specific area of your concern, and you defer to it. But, if authority gets overplayed, and the doctor or mechanic starts trying to shove a personal agenda down your throat, you often push back.

Such pushback manifests itself in less technical arenas, like our daily work. If your boss is an expert in a particular technology, and he sees every problem as having a solution that uses that particular technology, he might be tempted to beat you over the head with his technical solutions. Remember the old saying, "If you're a hammer, everything looks like a nail!" That supervisor's use of positional authority, if used frequently, will lead to resentment and pushback by whoever is getting pushed toward a particular answer. Authoritative leaders like to give advice and issue commands. To them the world remains a simple algorithm of problem-solution-result—and employees often look like problem-bearing platforms!

However, here's the REAL issue: There is often more than one solution to any problem, each with potential risks and rewards. Compounding this dilemma, we've all been conditioned to take problems to leaders, who are supposed to have all the answers.

Ironically, most people like autonomy and want to solve their own problems. Being told what to do often feels like being talked down to—especially if you have experience working with the problem or issue. This creates a dilemma: pressure for the leaders to "have the right/perfect answer" while people resent the very answers they get from their seemingly autocratic leaders. Thus, we've built a system that fosters authority-based leadership that no one really likes, but it's become the leadership default style in many organizations.

Here's the kicker about using authority as the principal mode of leadership: You have to employ surveillance! If employees receive an order, but are not convinced it's the right direction to take, they often engage in a behavior called "benign neglect"—hoping the leader's faulty direction will fade away like yesterday's news. If the leader fails to employ surveillance and enforcement, this benign neglect will dissipate the leader's command-and-control power. Furthermore, surveillance and enforcement require lots of time, money, and effort. Look at the cost of any occupational army in another country. The costs of being a top-down, command-and-control, authoritative leader far outweigh its benefits.

Questions, Not Answers

Great leaders avoid command and control; rather, they seek advice and consent. In short, great leaders are more focused on asking good questions than giving "the" right answers.

Such leaders respect the knowledge and experience of their followers. They start from a position of respect for the other person and assume some basic experience and knowledge. Obviously, if these assumptions prove inaccurate, they use coaching to solve that issue also, as quickly as possible.

What does a good question look like? Simple: It makes people stop, think, and reflect. A good question doesn't direct or even assume a direction; it's curious and exploratory. A good question does not rely on subject matter expertise, is open-ended rather than closed, and keeps people thinking, talking, and discovering. A good question comes from deep listening and responding to another person—not simply and politely waiting for a turn to talk and give advice!

Here are a few examples of questions both on and off the mark:

- What bothers you about how your boss is treating you?
  Not: So, it sounds like your boss is a jerk. That right?

[8]

- Explain what your boss actually does that annoys you. *Not:* I know it's annoying to have a bully for a boss; I've had the same experience—let me tell you about that.

- As an expert in your field, how do you feel when your boss doesn't listen to your suggestions? *Not:* I know that when I used to work at Smith and Jones, my boss never listened to me, and that just made me angry.

The Magic Sticky Note

It's one thing to learn, even to know, something but quite another to make what you've learned part of your life—your default practice. So, here's a simple way to learn the coach-approach to leadership—the Magic Sticky Note. To make your own, get a sticky (self-adhesive notepaper). A rectangular-shape, 2" x 3" if you write small, 3"x 5" or 4"x 6" if you don't, works best.

Step 1: Make your own Magic Sticky Note. On the left edge of the sticky note print the following four words:

- What?
- Who?
- How?
- Open-ended?

For starters, leave the rest of the note blank. There's more to come!

Now put the magic sticky note on the top of your desk and move it around every day. The varied location will disrupt your attention and remind you to use the questions. (Keeping the sticky note in the same place makes it part of the "background"—like wallpaper—and over time it goes unnoticed.)

Step 2. Practice asking questions. You should spend most of the next week practicing conversations with anyone you encounter by using those four questions: What? Who? How? Open-ended? The key is to ask questions and make the conversation all about the other person, not all about you!

Asking these kinds of questions, and not simply questions that can be answered with a "yes" or a "no," will give you a great jump-start on coaching.

This is much more difficult to do than you think—especially because our educational system rewards us for always having the right answers. To help you with this question-based approach, get really curious—as if you were interviewing people for a news article you'll have to write after the interview. Here's a simple, quick question-based, coach-approach conversation:

Amy: How's it going, Jack?

Jack: Okay, I guess.

Amy: You guess? So, what's happening?

Jack: My new boss and I don't get along.

Amy: How so?

Jack: Last week, he reassigned one of my assignments to another guy, without ever consulting me first.

Amy: What precipitated that?

Jack: The customer complained to him that I wasn't responsive.

Amy: What do you mean?

Jack: I was out of town and my cell battery went dead. The client sent me an urgent message. I couldn't get a new battery until later the next day. But the client panicked and called my boss and my boss overacted and reassigned the client. And now I'm losing a big commission check—over a dead cell battery.

Amy: What did your boss say when you told him about the battery?

Jack: Something flip, like I should anticipate problems. Unbelievable, like I should carry a spare cell battery in my back pocket!

Amy: So, what do you think you should do next?

Jack: Well, I need to cool off and then talk to my boss about reasonable expectations. And I'm going to call my old client and tell him what happened...I guess that's a place to start.

Amy: Sounds reasonable to me.

Jack: Thanks, Amy. I appreciate you just listening to me.

Notice that in the above conversation Amy offered no advice whatsoever. All she did was ask *What, Who, How,* and *Open-Ended* questions. Jack figured out next steps, not Amy. No advice, just good questions!

Step 3: Finish the magic sticky note. Take out your "magic sticky note" with the key questions on the left side. Then, sketch out what I call the coaching clock and the word CHANGE on the right side of the sticky. Here's what the final version of the sticky should look like:

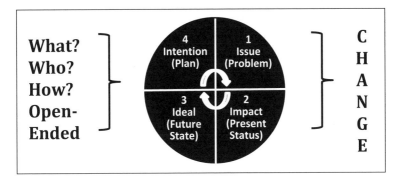

Step 4: Learn how the Coaching Clock works. You will use a "4-by-4 approach."

- The first "4" relates to the four key questions you ask (What? Who? How? Open-ended questions?). These four questions should be asked throughout the coach-approach conversation.

- The second "4" relates to the four-step coaching clock that represents the four phases of the coach-approach conversation.

The four phases of the coaching clock are called the 4-I's: (1) Issue causing a problem; (2) Impact of the present state; (3) Ideal state in the future; (4) Intention going forward to solve the problem.

1. **Issue:** As a coach-approach leader you can't help someone solve a problem unless and until you both know and agree on what the problem is. Sounds simple. But you'd be surprised by how many people and organizations rush to judgment and solve the WRONG problem. I can't recall a time when the reason prompting a client to come in for executive coaching turned out to be the real issue requiring attention. The initial conversation only represents a starting place. The real problem requires probing, asking questions and getting affirmation before going forward. I call that process "peeling the onion" to get below the surface level to the essence of the issue. Here are a few directions and questions to get started:

   a) Identify the behavior or issue to discuss.

      - What's the most important thing for us to discuss today?
      - Paraphrase the problem back to the person for agreement.

b) Determine the purpose or outcomes.

- What would you most like to accomplish in our conversation?

c) Agree on the process for the conversation.

- Here's how I thought we might proceed (here I describe the coaching clock)...What do you think?

2. **Impact:** The second phase of the coach-approach involves determining the impact of the "present" status of the issue or problem. In this phase of inquiry, the coach-approach leader tries to determine current state, extent, and impact of the issue on key stakeholders, especially the person with whom you're talking. In other words, the coach-approach leader determines how large or small, how immediate or remote, how expensive or cheap the problem is to solve. If you know the size and scope of the issue or problem, it gives you perspective to ask more helpful questions of the client to help resolve the issue. Here are a few directions and questions to get started in this phase:

a) Determine the present status of the issue or problem.

- Describe what the situation looks like today. What's going on?

b) Understand the person's perspective.

- How do you see this situation? On a scale from 1 to 10, how important is this to you?

c) Determine the consequences of continuing on the present path.

- What's the impact (emotional, financial, etc.) this is having on you? On others? Anyone else? What's the cost of doing nothing?

3. **Ideal State**: There have been a number of experiments about people using visioning to improve their skills. One involves shooting basketball foul shots. In this experiment, three groups were measured: one group practiced actually shooting lots of foul shots; another group did nothing; and a final group frequently envisioned shooting successful foul shots but never actually touched the ball until the final phase when all three groups were tested. The results: The highest-scoring people were the ones who actually practiced with the ball. However, coming in close second place was the group who envisioned taking shots. Finally, at the bottom of the heap were those who did not practice at all (nothing surprising).

This experiment, and much that we know about goal setting, teaches us that having an ideal state in mind before you go on the journey is not just a good idea, it's critical to success because it acts like a stake in the ground.

So, after you probe your employee or colleague to describe in detail what the impact of the present state of the issue or problem looks like, then you may want to ask some clarifying questions. These questions help people shift their thinking from what's wrong to what they really want. This shift is critical to finding a solution. Without the ideal "target" in mind, it's very difficult to hit that target. To clarify the ideal state, consider the following areas to probe and the questions associated with each:

a) Understand the vision for success.

- What would the ideal state look like?
- If a miracle happened overnight, what would it look like?

b) Set goals and performance expectations.

- What do you want to accomplish?

c) Identify possible barriers or resistance.

- What are the major barriers in your way?

d) Explore alternative paths of action.

- What are some different approaches/steps you might take?
- What else?

4. **Intention:** The final step in the coach-approach leader's process is to move the colleague/client/employee toward action. Remember: Good Coaching = Action. Therefore, no action, no coaching. It's not just about having a great conversation; rather, having a great conversation that moves the person to take steps toward solving an issue or problem. The key in this step is to be direct. Ask for a plan and for accountability while at the same time not overwhelming people. Start with this:

a) Agree on a first step moving us toward the goal.

- What will be your first...even easiest...step to take?

b) Enlist support from others.

- Who can support you going forward?

c) Set milestones and accountability.

- Where and when can you start?
- What's your timeline to complete the process?
- What do you want to be held accountable for?
- How will I know you've accomplished it?

When you and the client finish the coaching session, it's worth getting some feedback on your coaching. It's a bit like the maître-d stopping by your table and asking how you enjoyed the meal. Here are a few questions you might ask:

- How do you feel about today's session?

- What's one thing of value that you got from this discussion?

- Are there any questions you have or feedback you'd like to give me about today's meeting?

[15]

By now, I'm guessing you may be asking yourself: So, why does he call it the coaching clock?

Good question! And the answer is that all coaching takes time, and sometimes a leader's time is limited. The second reason is that most often people make their biggest errors by blasting through the issue or problem identification phase WAY too quickly. So, one purpose of the clock is to make phases of the process very intentional.

Let's now picture the clock process as if it were a clock— an analog clock.

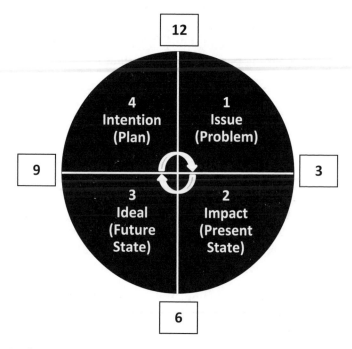

Let's assume you only have about 20 minutes to talk to a direct report about something that's bugging her. She comes into your office with a problem that she'd like you to "help" her with. Loosely translated, that often means she'd love to give you the problem to solve. However, rather than grab that sticky problem that will cling to you like Velcro, I'm going to ask you to develop very short "alligator arms." (If you've ever observed alligators, you'll recall that they have extremely short arms!) When anyone comes into the office and tries to give you a problem, think of the alligator with such short arms that it couldn't take a problem, even if it wanted to. Don't reach out to take on other people's problems. Rather, use the coach-approach to help them solve their own.

How does time work with the coaching clock? It's simple, straightforward, and effective. Let's say a direct report comes in and tries to drop a problem on you—a hit-and-run management issue. Let's also assume you have a meeting with your boss in the next half hour. Here's what you might consider doing with your employee:

- Invite her to sit down. Tell her you have about 20 minutes before you have to get ready for a meeting with your boss, but you want to help her.

- Divide the coaching clock into four equal sections of five minutes apiece. Then begin the questioning: "OK, so what's the problem or issue you want to talk about today?"

Especially, make sure that you spend at least five minutes to identify the "real" issue or problem. In fact, if you have to bias the time in one of the four areas, use more time in identifying the problem—always. The issue that people present initially is usually not the real issue (which will emerge with good, probing questions).

If you use the coaching clock to guide the process and to address the timing issue, it provides you with a near-perfect, problem-solving instrument.

To recap: Divide whatever time you have available to work with a client into four equal parts and devote one part to each phase of the coach-approach. But remember—it's most important to identify the real problem, even if you have to spend a bit more time doing so. Coming up with a great answer to the wrong problem is far worse than developing a partial answer to the right one.

[17]

How to Use the Coach-Approach Process

Question: So, when can you use coaching? **Answer:** Anywhere, anytime, with anyone.

You need not wait for the perfect time of the day, the perfect setting, or the perfect moment in your relationship. In fact, the more spontaneous and authentic the situation, the more powerful the process becomes.

Coaching Friends

To practice your coaching technique, try it out on a friend. However, don't tell your friend that you're practicing coaching—just do it. Ask "what, how, who" questions to get the ball rolling. Make it all about your friend and watch coaching start to work. Here's how it might go:

You: Hey Pete! What's up?

Pete: Not much.

You: Everything okay?

Pete: Sort of.

You: Sort of? What's that mean?

Pete: Well, Mary and I are arguing a lot these days.

You: About what?

Pete: The same old thing, money.

You: What about money?

Pete: I like to spend it and, well, Mary likes to save it.

At this point, you're well on your way to having a coaching conversation. Establish what the real issue or problem is, what the impact of the present status looks like, then find out the ideal state, and finally ask him his intention and to establish a plan and some sort of accountability for his actions.

One caveat with friends: When you get to the intention stage, my advice is to be low key about holding them accountable. So you might ask, "Would it help if you let me know how it went?" or "Hey, let me know how it goes when you talk to her." It's that easy. And, you can practice it all the time, anywhere—at work, at lunch, or at Starbucks.

The more you practice, the better you'll get. What seems awkward at first will blossom into a real skill over time. For most leaders, who are used to giving answers rather than asking questions, the first few tries are as hard as writing your name with your nondominant hand. Give that a try right now to anticipate how hard it will be. But with about a month's practice, you really get good at adapting to a new way of doing business. The practice forms new neural pathways—the more practice, the deeper the neural groove and more polished the skill.

A quick story about adapting to a new skill: Whenever I start writing a new book, I write at least several hours a day for about three months. That's done after having researched my topic for six months to a year. But when the writing comes, if I'm not careful, I'll develop tendinitis in my right arm and often in my shoulder. When it first happened, I had an exam and an MRI only to eventually determine from a friend that I just needed to switch my computer mouse from my right to my left hand—to rest my right arm and shoulder. And, I hated it! It felt like my left hand was rented from someone else. Every click and motion took f-o-r-e-v-e-r. But after a month of struggling with using my left hand, I've become so proficient that I can switch hands at will. In fact, when people see me working, they often ask if I'm left-handed. And the best part: No more shoulder pains.

Coaching Direct Reports

Coaching direct reports might be the next best place to practice. Again, at first, you need not announce that you're actually coaching them. However, don't be surprised if they notice the difference in the way you're treating them, especially if you've been a very directive, top-down-authoritarian boss in the past. Oftentimes, people will wonder what's going on simply because you're acting so differently. Remember: People are exquisitely attuned to changes and variances from the norm, especially if the difference is stark, like going from giving answers to asking questions.

The coaching conversation can also be initiated when someone comes into your office with a problem and wants to "give" you that problem. Remember: Develop "alligator arms" and go into coaching mode ("So, can you tell me what the problem is?"). Consider how much time you have, look down at the Magic Sticky Note on your desk, and use the "coaching clock" to recall the four phases of coaching (the 4-I's—Issue, Impact, Ideal, Intention). Also, use the "clock" to apportion your timeline for the meeting. This time when you come to the intention, plan, and accountability stage, absolutely ask the person to get back to you. This does several things. They know you care. They know they have to do something. And, they'll think twice about bringing in every problem, trying to drop it on your doorstep!

Coaching Peers

When you want to step up from family and direct reports, give peers a try. Remember, you don't need or want to announce that you'll be coaching them. Just engage them in conversation by asking "What's up?" or "How's it going?" or "What's going on these days?" Any open-ended question allows them to respond. The key is to listen and watch their responses. If they say "fine," "OK," or "So, so," then you might want to probe them further. You might ask, "Wanna talk about whatever's happening?" Just know that anyone who says that life is "fine" or "OK" is not living in the "sweet spot" of life by any stretch of the imagination. Quite the opposite, in fact.

Use the coaching clock to ensure that you stick to the process and that you'll spend time in each stage of the model—especially establishing what the real issue or problem is. At the end of the conversation, you might hint that if they come up with a plan, you'd really like to know when they did whatever they promised to do. I'd keep it casual but try to get some feedback going, without making it feel forced or aggressive.

Coaching Your Boss

This kind of coaching might well be the trickiest—and the most rewarding. Everyone in the world needs a sounding board, and the better a listener you become by applying the coach-approach process, the more likely you can help fill that sounding-board role even for your own boss. Just because someone is in charge, it doesn't mean you can't coach her or him. Again, the first step is asking the opening question: "What's going on?" or "How's the XYZ account going?" Then you follow up with more questions to clarify the issue or problem, the impact of the current status, the ideal state, and the intention around the problem and accountability factors going forward. The first couple of times you give the coach-approach a try with your boss, keep it low-key and very conversational, not at all lockstep structured. Otherwise, you could lose her trust early on.

Becoming a trusted sounding board will put you in the middle of important decisions, including ones that may affect your own future. And the best way to get to that coveted place is through authentic curiosity, probing questions, and reflective listening—using the coach-approach.

Coaching Clients and Developing Business

One of the best uses of the coach-approach comes when you're working with established clients or developing new business and new clients. So, the next time you're at an event or a social gathering try this approach:

1. Most often, the person hosting the event knows the business interests of most people coming to an event—so you might ask him or her which people might be good connections for you. Knowing this can

[21]

focus your time and attention and acts like an excellent prospecting tool.

2. Set some limits. Let's assume that you'd like to meet three critical people whom the host has pointed out to you. And let's also assume that you have about an hour to stay at the event. Thus, you have about 20 minutes to spend with each new prospect.

3. Walk up to someone you might want to meet and introduce yourself. Then allow the person to do the same. Ask about their company.

4. Next, apply the coaching clock. You have 20 minutes and must use them wisely. Remember the 4-I's—and start the discussion by asking, "So in your company, what's one of the biggest issues you're facing?"

5. When the person tells you the issue, probe this issue by asking Who? What? How? and Open-Ended questions. When you think you know the important issue, paraphrase it to test whether or not you have it right. Don't proceed further until you do.

6. Next, employ the second "I" (of the 4-I's) and ask about the impact of the present situation (on this issue). What's the financial, social, emotional impact it's having on the company and on the prospect? Try to establish its "pain" priority for the person and the company.

7. Next, to the third "I"—the Ideal State. Ask what the ideal state would look like if it were possible. Probe this to get a very accurate and detailed description, and don't let them undercut themselves by putting down their own ideal state by saying, "Yeah, but that's not happening." Stick close to the ideal state.

8. Next, the fourth "I"—Intention. Here's where there's a slight variance. When you listen to the problem, consider if there's someone in your company who

could help them. Or, perhaps there's another company that you could refer, knowing that it might be a good fit. Even if you have no idea how to help, just listening so intently focused on the problem will elicit the person's good thoughts—and the possibility of recommending you to someone she/he knows.

9. After you've heard someone articulate a major problem, you've provided a great service, one that won't soon be forgotten. And, following such a coach-approach experience, your prospect will most likely WANT to hear about your company. Consider that people who ask you about what your company does put you in a very strong position—all because you used the coach-approach and showed that you cared about your prospect and your prospect's business. She/he reciprocates by listening to you.

How to Use the Coach-Approach with Teams

Much has been written on the power of groups, the wisdom of crowds, and the liabilities associated with groupthink. Coaching won't cure all the issues associated with teams and the variety of gatherings of people because so much depends on their intergroup relationships, the power differential between individual members, the overarching corporate culture, and other complex factors. However, a coach can ask the entire team important questions to leverage the team's collective intelligence.

At some point, all of us work in teams; it's the basis for any organization to scale its operations and leverage diversity. Teams produce software, build houses, change business processes, and win or lose football games. And while you may wish to distinguish between ad hoc teams or intact teams, when you work on a team both good things and challenges arise. You get more good things:

- Options
- Brain Power
- Perspective
- Acceptance

You also get more challenges:

- Power plays
- Politics
- Arguments
- Complexity

So, like most good options, teams come at a certain price. The trick is to maximize team benefits and minimize team liabilities. Using the coach-approach helps us capitalize on the benefits, as well as recognize and even avoid the liabilities. In the following pages, we'll explore Leadership Flash (LF) team coaching and Leadership Action-Learning (LAL) team coaching.

Leadership Flash Team Coaching

Companies and organizations get hit with challenges every day. Some are more significant than others and only require an expert to supply an answer to meet that challenge. Think of it like calling a help desk when a glitch happens with your computer. You call an expert (tech support) to help you get your e-mail back up and running, to unstick a program, or get your new mouse to work with your operating system. And for the most part, it's just a call, an answer, and your challenge gets solved.

But what happens when the problem is immediate, urgent, and complex? You need to bid on a proposal in the next 48 hours or lose the opportunity; or you're coming up on a deadline to revamp or leave in place a broken business development model. Both questions mean real money and success or failure for your organization.

How do you address these situations on a timely basis without making a hasty decision that will cost you a lot down the road? Before answering that, consider the research of Daniel Kahneman, Nobel prize-winning psychologist. Kahneman discovered that we employ two modes of thinking and decision making: System 1—thinking fast (intuitive) and System 2—thinking slow (rational). Most of our decision making is done by our intuition. It's done quickly, often works well (especially when we're practiced in an area), but also exposes us to untold biases. For example, consider Mary, a bright young girl who could read fluently at age 4. Can you predict her cumulative point average in college, years later? Chances are better than even that your estimates would be closer to a 4.0 than not. The truth is, Mary's cumulative average is more likely to be closer to a 3.0, but the mere mention of the number 4 (the age she could read and that reading at age 4 indicates a precocious child) biases our thinking such that we consider her a 4.0 student. Kahneman's newest book *Thinking Fast and Slow* is well worth the read.

Biases like these operate when we make decisions. Unfortunately, when you buy a house, a car, or even choose a vacation, you're often disproportionately biased by the asking price, which sets your anchor and influences your "intuition" without your knowing it.

Now, back to the immediate, urgent business challenge: How can you slow down this quick-thinking process so you can make better, more informed decisions under the pressure of a deadline? You gather a team, and you use the coach-approach.

A team of diverse, knowledgeable, engaged team members using this process to address a known and important topic can collectively come up with a much better solution than any single person, even a very smart person such as an expert. Teams can beat smart people because the coach-approach process engages the team's collective intelligence by posting a flashing yellow caution light to the racing brain, slowing it down. The diversity of team members offers a variety of views to attack the problem. The team can do this efficiently and effectively, even under pressure, if led by a knowledgeable coach.

Here's the process:

- Gather a team (four to eight people) with a particular issue that is not a simple problem but an important and urgent one. Fewer than four people and you lose the power of the collective intelligence; having more than eight team members scrambles the process with too much noise and too complicated a set of logistics coordinating such large teams. Be sure the team members have general knowledge about the issue and a stake in its solution. You will also want to consider other factors like diversity (gender, race, etc.) and direct experience with the topic.

- On the other hand, you might have an intact team that has to solve the problem, where both choice and variety might be limited. In either case, engage a coach (neutral, experienced, and trained) to help guide the team through the process.

- Next, set the rules. In this case, because you need answers quickly but want the collective wisdom of the crowd, the coach will use the following process: Ask questions (what, who, how, and open-ended) of the group, making sure that extroverts don't dominate; ask each person, in sequence, his/her thoughts; then open up the meeting for broader discussion—always in response to questions.

- The coach's job in leadership flash team coaching is to keep the process going: to ask questions, manage the process, and engage the entire team. She/he can question the group as if it were a person, invite others to ask questions, and move the process through the key questions (Who? What? How? Open-Ended?) and through the 4-I's (Issue, Impact, Ideal, Intention).

- The coach will use the coaching clock to guide the group through the four stages of the 4-I's, and the team will decide on an intentional action plan and accountability going forward—what needs to get done and who will do it.

Let's see how this might work in a specific situation, for instance when you get an imminent deadline from a large organization that needs a proposal in two days. This is a perfect time to gather the team (most suited to the proposal) and have a Leadership Flash (LF) team coaching session.

Issue or Problem Stage

The coach will probe the group during this initial phase with questions (What, Who, etc.) to fully identify and explore the nature of the issue or problem, before ever attempting to get the team to solve the problem. It's best to be generous with time during this phase, perhaps even spending the first hour or more on problem identification. Remember: An elegant, even perfect solution to the wrong problem is not nearly as effective as an adequate solution to the right issue or problem.

Note that while the coach might start probing in a linear way, asking what is the problem, who is involved, etc., the coach might also ask questions in a way that invites the person to provide more and more information about one question, information that might be "associative," or nonlinear. For example, as the coach, you might ask what someone thinks and follow up directly by asking the person to describe it for you. Also, note that while the coach can move the process along by asking questions, anyone in the group should ask questions as well. Questions will always trump statements.

During this process, the coach might use a flip chart but also ask someone else to keep notes. Also, the coach's role is to stimulate diversity of thought and keep the discussion moving—much as she/he would do when coaching an individual. However, the more engaged the group gets at asking questions, the richer the discussion. Here are some questions that might get asked in the discussion:

1. What does the customer really want? What sorts of requests like this one have you addressed before from this customer? What issues or problems have you encountered before with this customer? What else? What else?

2. With whom would you be working on the customer side? Who are the best people in your company to pull this proposal together and can you take them off their current assignments to address this one? Who else should be considered? Who else? Who else?

3. How reasonable is it to expect that you can have the proposal done in 48 hours? How have you success-fully addressed problems like this in the past? How might you start to look at this particular one?

4. Can anyone explain the major issues involved in this proposal? Help me understand what you said. Can you go into that in more depth? So, can you describe what that would look like?

Impact of the Issue

The coach now moves to the impact of the present state and asks the same four questions to attempt to get a clear picture of the size of the problem, its impact on the company (financial, emotional, cultural, etc.). Here is a sample of such questions, in no particular order:

- So, how do you all feel about the value of this proposal to the company?

- On a scale from 1–10 (1=low and 10=high) how do you rank this in importance to your company?

- If you pass on this and walk away from the proposal, what is the impact on all concerned and on the company? What else? What else?

- Can someone explain where you stand regarding our revenue targets for the quarter and for the entire year?

Once the coach feels that the team has asked good questions and has done a sufficient job identifying a clear picture of the impact of the current state, the coach moves the team toward the "ideal" or best possible state.

Ideal State

The coach next asks the team to envision the ideal state so they have a clear, direct path toward the future. Again, asking the what, who, how, and open-ended questions, the coach probes the vision for the future. Here are some questions that might emerge from both the team and/or the coach, in no particular order:

- If a magic wand hit us overnight and gave us an ideal solution, what would that look like?

- What does the ideal proposal for this project look like?

- Who can envision at least one key future state for this proposal?

- Let's say you hit this proposal out of the park. Can you describe what that would look like and what you would have done?

Intention—Plan and Accountability

Next, the coach asks the team to develop a plan and asks to what standard each team member wants to be held accountable in the next 24 hours. Again, asking the what, who, how, and open-ended questions, the coach moves the team toward their intention about completing the proposal on time, in an excellent manner, and holding members accountable for specific responsibilities. Some questions that might emerge from the team and the coach:

- How should this proposal look going forward?
- Who can take a stab at the key steps in front of us?

- What are the top three things we must do now?
- What would a timeline look like?
- Who here would volunteer for what deliverable, and by when?

The coach then asks the note-taker to write up the meeting, paying particular attention to the timeline, deliverables, and assignments. Also, the coach calls for a follow-up meeting the next day or even for later that day, depending on tasks and time sensitivity.

This Leadership Flash team coaching takes advantage of collective intelligence, a strong coach-approach methodology, and an experienced coach. The results are much better decisions, higher-quality products in a shorter time frame, and better team buy-in to the product or service. Remember Kahneman's caution not to let the fast-thinking emotional brain hijack the rational brain. Slow down the process by providing a process that is rational and deliberative, one that employs diversity and exploits collective intelligence.

What happens when the problem is much larger, longer-term, and of great impact financially and culturally to the company? In that case, employ Leadership Action Learning team coaching.

Leadership Action Learning (LAL) Team Coaching

Now we turn to long-term problems that have no particular "correct" solution, but the solution of which has an important impact on the organization or person. Think of this problem as a much more strategic, often long-term problem. In Leadership Action Learning (LAL) team coaching, the issue is important but not urgent—unlike issues in Leadership Flash team coaching, which are both important AND urgent.

Here's a typical LAL problem: Your business development (BD) model, which worked when there was little competition, is beginning to sputter and threatens to no longer produce the level of revenue required to sustain your company's long-term market share. This is a very important issue. While not immediately urgent, if it's not addressed systematically and strategically, it will eventually lead to the company's undoing. This is the perfect time to use LAL team coaching, which is based on a process called Action Learning.

First, a brief history of Action Learning: Physicist Reg Ravens worked at the famous Cavendish Labs in England. Ravens observed how Nobel Prize-winning scientists in these renowned research labs humbly used questions to help each other discover breakthrough scientific discoveries. This inquiry process helped Ravens frame the basis for what he called Action Learning—a process that uses questions, wisdom, and respect rather than answers, expertise, and power or status to help people figure out answers to difficult questions and, at the same time, to learn important interpersonal and leadership skills in the process.

Action Learning proved to be so powerful that a growing number of companies—for example, GE, AT&T, Corning, Whirlpool, GTE, Motorola, Coca Cola, Dow, Exxon—are now using it to resolve major corporate issues or problems. Currently, the Action Learning gurus in the United States are Professor Steve Marquardt and his colleagues at George Washington University. Marquardt has written and spoken extensively on the topic of Action Learning. Moreover, he and his colleagues have started the World Institute for Action Learning (WIAL; http://www.wial.org/).

Action Learning has some fundamental requirements and can be used by anyone to solve problems, especially when everyone on the team involved is not necessarily an expert in the area. I use the term Leadership Action Learning team coaching because the instances where I see Action Learning best applied are in the leadership arena, where things get done as a team in a sustainable way that moves corporate and government agendas forward.

Leadership Action Learning Coaching Requirements

There are some basic requirements to enable effective Leadership Action Learning team coaching. They are as follows:

- A team of four to eight people who need not be experts in the problem area.

- A coach with experience in leading Action Learning groups.

- A problem that has no single solution but is important to the organization.

- Use of an inquiry model using powerful questions that require reflection, listening, and respect. Key questions: Who, What, How, and Open-Ended questions.

- A bias for taking action.

The Leadership Action Learning team coaching process (along with Action Learning) has only a few salient rules:

- A statement or pronouncement can only be made if responding to a question.

- The coach has authority over the ground rules, the process, and learning. The coach can stop and start the process but does not participate in the solution itself.

- Thus, the coach owns the process, and the team owns the content.

I believe that Leadership Action Learning team coaching should take the Action Learning process through the same guided coaching process (key questions and the 4-I's) that I suggested in the individual coaching process and in the Leadership Flash team coaching. However, when using this model with a team, all of whom might not be experts but who possess wisdom and experience, the key element that provokes reflection and learning will always be the questions asked *by participants*. In fact, having a group of experts trying to solve an issue is not always the best use of team action learning.

The nonexpert often asks the most the most insightful questions, precisely because she/he is not an expert.

At its heart, Leadership Action Learning team coaching not only produces solutions to issues or problems but also teaches people the most important skills of great leaders: humility, listening, asking the right questions, and the will to take action. A quick note here about Jim Collins' research in his bestselling book, *Good to Great*. Collins found that the greatest leaders of all time in American business had two surprising characteristics: (1) a strong will to get things done and (2) humility—not procrastination and arrogance.

Leadership Action Learning Process Overview

Here's what the Leadership Action Learning team coaching process might look like:

1. The coach will ask a person with a problem to present or explain what she/he thinks is the problem or issue. Generally, the presenter should take no more than about five minutes to lay out the problem. Then, the team should be allowed to ask questions of the presenter (and themselves) to help the team, and often even the presenter, better understand and refine the core problem.

2. After about 15 minutes, the coach will stop the proceedings to see if everyone—including the problem presenter—really understands the problem. At this point in the conversation, experienced coaches ask each team member to write down a description of the problem. Then the coach invites each member to read the description to the problem owner. If you skip this step or simply do it orally, people get lazy and follow the herd and say things like, "I agree with what Sam said." Independent, diverse thinking contributes far more at this stage. Have team members write it down and read it. Some coaches use sticky notes and others index cards for this process.

[33]

3. Next, it's useful to see how close the team is to understanding the *real* problem—a most critical point in the process. Einstein once said, "If I had an hour to solve a problem and my life depended on the solution, I would spend the first 55 minutes determining the proper question to ask, for once I know the proper question, I could solve the problem in less than five minutes." Often, highly driven and motivated people—all chomping at the bit—just want to solve problems, regardless of whether or not they completely understand the problem. Thus, they want to come up with answers because that's the competitive behavior that made them successful in the past. My personal warning to such overachievers comes in the form of a book title of a colleague, Marshall Goldsmith: *What Got You Here Won't Get You There!*

4. If (in the mind of the problem owner) the team has not hit the problem squarely, the coach should put the team back to work and do another discovery round until the problem owner is convinced that the team has its focus on the real problem at hand. Remember that often even the problem owner isn't clear and the team inquiry helps him or her to better understand the real problem. In essence, problem identification is essential and iterative.

5. Note that the team's inquiry process (i.e., how the team interrogates the problem) should use the very same questions used in individual coaching: What, who, how, and open-ended questions. Again, it's critical that these questions get asked, rather than "yes-no" questions or directive questions (for example, "Have you thought of trying the XYZ process?"). Directive questions narrow thinking too quickly and can often quickly solve the wrong problem! Recall another Albert Einstein quote about problem solving: "We can't *solve problems* by using the same kind of thinking we used when we created them."

6. Once the issue or problem is clear, the coach leads the group through the other three stages outlined in the coaching clock with particular attention to allocating at least the same amount of time on problem identification as any other of the four stages (Issue, Impact, Ideal, and Intention). Note, again: Teams should err on the side of spending more time clarifying the problem. And, while the coach may pose or introduce each of the quadrants of the coaching clock to keep the team on track, the coach does not engage in problem solving, only in guiding the process.

7. When the team coaching session ends, the coach asks team members what they learned about leadership in general. Regarding leadership, participants will often comment on how they learned to really listen, to respect others' opinions, and to be more patient. All these and other lessons are terrific for leadership maturity. Another way of asking a similar question more indirectly is to ask: "What one or two things of value did you get from today's team meeting?"

8. The coach then will ask each person what she/he will do before the next meeting. It's important that everyone be invested—i.e., that everyone takes actions that move the team toward solutions. In essence, the team owns the problem and so all must work to solve it. Usually, people step up and offer to do some research, make some calls, interview or survey people in their own areas of responsibility, and report back at the next meeting.

One note about notes! Early on the coach will ask someone from the group to consider taking notes. Certainly, the coach should indicate that each time someone else will take a turn at note taking.

Follow-Up to Leadership Action Learning Meetings

In follow-up meetings, the coach might start with an opening round where each person reports what she/he found after engaging in research and inquiry. After the reports are finished, it's a good idea to test the problem to check if it's remained the same or if it's changed based on the research. The coach might ask the team to restate the problem concisely as they now see it, even to write it down and read it out loud. If there's a new finding or twist on the issue, it's worth spending time making sure the problem gets re-clarified before diving back into solutions. The coach might also ask the Present Status or Impact of the problem—how is it going, and has it gotten worse, better, or about the same? Note that the coach is essentially going back over the coaching clock perhaps more quickly or slowly depending upon how the group responds. There's no "normal" and the coach works with wherever the group finds itself.

Next, the coach gets the team to address the Ideal State again. Has that changed? What are the priorities given the new findings that team members brought back to the table? Note that the coach can stop and start the group based on what she/he senses is needed to make the process work for the team. For example, whenever I see a group get stuck, sometimes I'll say, "OK, it feels like we're stuck on this point. Would you all like to take a break and brainstorm for 10 minutes?" Or, "How about taking out a piece of paper and writing down how you're feeling right now? Please be as honest as possible."

Toward the end of each session with a Leadership Action Learning team, the coach should do the following:

1. Ask each team member what she/he will do before the next meeting to help address the problem.

2. Ask team members to describe how the session was of value in solving the problem.

3. Ask team members what leadership insights they are gleaning from the process (like listening, asking questions, reflecting more, being less judgmental, becoming a better follower, etc.).

4. Set the dates and times for the follow-up meetings. All should have their calendars handy.

Special note: To be sure, teams can run into problems, such as members who don't show and people who don't contribute. There are ways to deal with such bothersome issues, but always the best way will be for the coach to "call the issue" whatever it is and ask the group how they want to deal with it. For example, if Joe hasn't attended the meetings, then the coach might say: "I notice that Joe hasn't shown up to the past two meetings. Should we discuss this as a team?" Teams are very capable of solving problems, and coaches have to be willing to live with team solutions.

Conclusion

The coach-approach to leadership will not cure cancer! But it will solve some pretty cancerous problems that can hurt or even destroy individuals and companies.

Using the coach approach for leaders and their teams isn't just a neat idea, it's one of the most important leadership team insights. Asking key questions—What, Who, How, and Open-Ended?—and weaving those questions around the Coaching Clock process of the 4-I's (Issue—Impact—Ideal—Intention) ensures the rigor and structure that support an important problem-solving process. In the end, a group of dedicated, smart people can solve a problem better than any one expert could ever hope to, regardless of his or her credentials.

Part II
The Story

Chapter 1
The Interview

Dragging his right foot a bit, the frail, elderly gentleman walked into the conference room of a gleaming office building in Arlington, Virginia, across from the Ballston Mall and right next to the National Science Foundation. Comfortably dressed for the late spring weather in a dark blue suit of tropical wool, white shirt, and striped tie, the balding man smiled warmly at Margaret Thomas, who at 27 years old was still young enough to be his grandchild. She matched his smile instantly, pushed back her long blond hair over her narrow shoulders, and rose to greet him.

She was athletic, trim, and at 5'7" stood at least an inch taller than her guest. "Hello, are you Mr. Bausch?" she said.

"Leon, please. Leon Bausch," he said.

She ushered him to one of the four seats at the circular mahogany table, helping him into the chair like she had done for her grandfather so many times, just enough aid to be helpful without embarrassing him. Then she pointed to the array of juice, coffee, tea, and assorted pastries, saying, "May I get you anything, Mr. Bausch?"

"Leon, please," he said. "No thank you."

"Well, ah, Leon, we'll be joined by my boss and another senior manager from our consulting practice in just a minute or two."

"How long have you worked here?" Leon asked.

"Next week, it will be six months."

"And how's it going?"

"Great."

"How's your boss?"

"Well, you'll get a chance to meet her soon," Margaret said looking around. "In fact, here she comes right now."

Irene Murphy was also tall and attractive, her blond hair pulled back into a bun. Dressed in a tailored suit, she walked into the room, heading straight for the refreshments. "Margaret, I asked for chai tea," she said.

"I'm sorry, Ms. Murphy. I can run to Starbucks downstairs if you want me to. I forgot to ask the caterers. I'm so sorry."

Irene swung her head around with such force that her earrings hit the side of her face, but when she saw Leon, she pulled back and said, "We'll discuss that later. And, who is this gentleman?"

"Leon," Margaret said.

"Leon?" Irene responded.

With that, Leon pushed back his chair and struggled to his feet, stuck out his hand, and introduced himself.

"You're Leon Bausch?" she said, now staring at the résumé she held. "You're the applicant for the senior consultant position?"

"Yes, is there any problem?"

Irene hesitated for a second or two, as if she were doing some mathematical computation. "No, it's just that I was expect—"she stopped short, as if a baseball coach were giving her hand-and-arm signals to stay put. "No, I... well, we have one more manager, Rob Passis, who'll also be joining us. I hope soon," she said, checking her watch.

Leon nodded toward Irene and sat back down. Irene turned her attention back to the refreshments, fixed an Earl Grey tea for herself, and cut a small roll in half.

At 9:17 after some idle chit chat, Rob Passis breezed into the room, papers in hand, his wrinkled sports coat flapping, tie undone. "Hey, Irene and Margaret, sorry if I'm late."

"Again," said Irene.

Rob smiled, got himself coffee and food, then sat down at the table and introduced himself. "Haven't seen you before," he said to Leon. "What department are you from?"

"He's the applicant, Rob," Irene said.

"Oh," Rob said, "Can you give me a minute just to look over your résumé? Busy these days."

Leon nodded and smiled, Margaret looked down at her notes, and Irene scowled. After several minutes Rob spoke. "Thanks. Impressive. Harvard undergraduate and Yale Law School. I noticed you didn't include the years you attended."

"I didn't think I was required to."

"No. No. Of course not, Mr. Bausch," Irene said while her eyes shot out venom at Rob.

"Let's get started, shall we," Irene said. "Leon, can you tell us a little about yourself?"

"Well, I practiced law for 35 years with Bailey, Bausch, and Johnston. Did mostly corporate work."

"Cool. So why'd you leave?" Rob asked.

"I didn't. I'm still a partner there."

"But you want to join our company, too?" Rob said.

"Well, let's say I'm looking around for a new adventure."

"OK," Irene said. "The position is senior consultant for our corporate and federal practice. Mostly we work with the federal government. We've just been purchased by LBC, a holding company. So, how do you think you'd be a good fit for our firm?"

"First I'm a stockholder in the federal government. I pay my taxes every year."

Margaret smiled, then covered her smile with her hands.

"I presume we all pay our taxes, Mr. Bausch. Aside from that?"

"Yes, sorry, of course. But I've learned a lot about both the federal government and companies from all my legal work."

"Can you give us an example, Leon?" Rob asked before Irene could follow up.

"Well, I've negotiated contracts with the federal government, helped set up dozens of government contractors, and worked in M and A."

"M and A?" Margaret asked.

"Mergers and Acquisitions," Irene said.

"Yes, roughly two-thirds of them never work," Leon said as a footnote to Irene's comment.

"Really," said Rob.

The questions went on from there: Why do you want to become a management consultant? Why did you choose Pacific? What added value do you bring the company? All of these questions Leon answered professionally and as casually as if he were talking to someone he'd just met on the bus ride home.

Finally, Irene asked, "Do you have any questions for us?"

"Just one. And if each of you would answer it, that would be helpful to me."

"Fire away," Irene said, tapping her foot on the base of the table.

"What do you like about Pacific Consulting? And why?" he asked.

"To clarify," Irene said," that's two questions."

"OK, two questions."

She seemed disappointed, but said, "Excellent clients—a real 'who's who' stable. A great corporate stepping stone for the future," Irene said without hesitation.

Leon looked at Rob, who seemed to be half-dozing. "How about you, Rob?"

"Jeeze, I 'm sorry, what was the question again?"

"What do you like about Pacific?" Irene said with enough flint on her words to help a Boy Scout start a fire in the woods.

"The coffee and free food," he said, holding up a scone and smiling.

Leon smiled and turned to Margaret, "And how about you, Margaret?"

"Well, I'm not sure I'm the best one to ask. I've only been here six months."

"That's long enough," Leon said.

"It's the people I like the most: my colleagues. I've had a chance to work and learn a lot about business. I was an English major, so I'm kinda dumb about business," she said.

"I'd agree," Irene said, smiling, "but she's at least trying. I'll give her that much credit."

Margaret blushed and looked down at the papers in front of her.

"Any more questions, Mr. Bausch?" Irene asked, looking at her watch.

"No thank you, Ms. Murphy, I appreciate your candor."

"Fine, well, nice to meet you," Irene said. She stood up, shook his hand, and walked toward the door.

Rob ate the rest of the third muffin he'd attacked during the meeting, wiped his mouth, and stuck out his hand. "Great to meet you, Leonard."

"Leon."

"Right, Leon," he said, and headed toward the Danish before leaving the room.

Margaret sat with Leon as she collected her notes slowly and said, "Mr. Bausch, I'm..." She paused to think. "It's probably not my place to say this."

"Go ahead."

"I'm sorry."

"About what?"

"The way they acted. I'm afraid..."

"Don't worry. I'm used to that by now. You live long enough and your own kids start talking down to you."

"I'm just not proud," she stopped short.

As she spoke, Leon wrote a brief note on one piece of paper and then another. He dated, signed, and folded both of them. On one, he wrote Irene's name; on the other, he wrote Rob's name.

"Margaret, could you do me a favor?"

"Of course."

"I'd like you to deliver these notes when we're finished. Would you do that?"

"Sure."

He pushed the two folded notes in Margaret's direction.

"Next, I wonder if you'd like to work directly for me as my special assistant."

"What?"

"As I mentioned, my name is Leon Bausch. I own LBC." He waited.

"The same LBC that just purchased our consulting practice?"

"Yes. Leon Bausch Companies."

"I'm making some changes starting today," he said tapping both of the two termination notes he'd just written, "I'll be needing some help."

"Of course, Mr. Bausch."

"Leon," he said with a smile.

Chapter 2
The Gathering

Two weeks to the day after Leon told Margaret that he was the new owner of Pacific Consulting and asked her to become his special assistant, J.C. Williams walked into the Pacific reception area of its executive offices on the 12th floor. J.C. was tall—about 6'3"—trim and athletic. The year before, J.C. had resigned from the Darden Business School at the University of Virginia, where he had been informally voted by the MBA students as the hippest professor at Darden. Dressed in a blue blazer and a blue-and-white striped, crisply-starched, open-collar shirt, he pushed back his sandy brown hair as he walked toward Margaret. "You must be Dr. Williams," she said, smiling.

"J.C.," he said extending his right hand. His smile revealed a slight space between his almost perfect front teeth and his pale blue eyes were open and welcoming.

"Hi, I'm Margaret, Mr. Bausch is expecting you," she said, shaking his hand. She offered him some coffee, then ushered J.C. into Leon's office, where Leon embraced J.C. more like a nephew than a business associate.

"Margaret, J.C.'s the best executive coach in the country."

"Marshall Goldsmith might have a word or two to say about that," J.C. said with a grin.

"Point well taken," Leon said.

"Well, I'll leave you two alone. Nice to meet you, J.C."

"My pleasure, Margaret."

Leon told J.C. his take on the company after doing all the financial due diligence—that it was fundamentally sound but without a compelling vision or sense of purpose. People were professional, competent; their business pipeline was sufficient; but he didn't sense that they were a team focused on working together for something greater than themselves.

Both Leon and J.C. had worked together in several other business endeavors Leon had owned, so they could talk in deft shorthand.

J.C. asked, "On a scale from 1 to 5—low to high—how would you rate their level of emotional intelligence?"

"I'd say a 3. Most are self-aware and in control of their emotions. Just not sure they like each other or have the kind of empathy for colleagues and direct reports needed."

J.C. asked a number of other questions and quickly got the sense that the team was competent but uncaring toward each other or toward their mission.

About an hour later, J.C. emerged from Leon's office. He said goodbye to Margaret, after she set up another appointment on Leon's calendar for a meeting between him and J.C. just prior to the all-employee gathering a week hence.

At the gathering, Leon leaned on a podium in front of all 75 employees in the building's atrium, the morning sun streaming in. Standing off to the side was J.C. Williams.

Leon thanked everyone for coming, then cleared his throat and said, "I want to introduce a friend and my executive coach, J.C. Williams. I've relied on his guidance and confidence in my prior businesses and will use him to help me as I try to be the best CEO I possibly can be at Pacific."

Leon then presented J.C.'s biography. He'd been a Rhodes Scholar from Harvard, earned an MBA at the University of Chicago, and received his Ph.D. in business from Stanford before joining the faculty at the University of Virginia's Darden Business School. After leaving Darden several years ago to pursue a career as an executive coach, J.C. had become a national figure in the field, publishing and speaking on the value of coaching to the bottom line. "In short," Leon said, "J.C. is a leadership superstar."

Leon explained that he'd been studying the market and had found Pacific an excellent long-term investment, as much for the employees as the client base. "I believe that the company belongs to the employees, not the owner," Leon said. "Actually, we, you and I, all own this organization. I'm a simple man and believe that companies are just relationships within and outside the company. No relationships, no company." As he paused to take a sip of water, Leon noticed a number of smiling faces. He smiled back and continued discussing his years of working at other companies and about what employees had taught him. He told a couple of stories—mostly related to how he would have made mistakes—big ones—had some line employees not helped him see his own blind spots.

"Let me tell you about one last time I almost blew it big!" People chuckled, and again Leon paused to take a sip of water.

"So, at the time about 20 years ago, I smoked. Pretty stupid, I know. But one day I'm smoking outside the machine shop I used to run. One of my fellow smokers was the janitor and maintenance guy, Jerry."

Leon described how the company was having trouble with its manufacturing system. On a smoke break, he'd mentioned to Jerry that the company could not produce enough of the electric switches fast enough for the federal government—their prime customer. Jerry asked Leon if he'd mind being asked some questions. After listening to Leon awhile, Jerry began to get a sense of the problem and asked Leon if he would like an observation. Leon nodded, and Jerry offered his approach: Move a couple of pieces of machinery around to shortcut some sticking points.

Later, Leon gave Jerry's idea to one of his engineers. The engineer worked with Jerry and solved the problem in a few weeks, saving the company millions by being able to retain the lucrative government contract.

"That's when I discovered how smart everyone around me was, and how handicapped I was!" A healthy laugh arose from the collective crowd.

"My philosophy is simple: Teams of people are much smarter than any one person. I call it Team Wisdom," Leon continued. "And, the more diverse the members, the wiser the team gets. So, my approach to problem solving is to use what I call the coach-approach to problem solving. Whenever we have a big problem, I'll come to you for answers. It's that simple."

With that, Leon turned to J.C. and said, "Now, I want to let J.C. explain how simple and effective this approach is, because he's the one who taught me about it," he said and handed the mike to J.C., who had walked up to the podium next to Leon.

"Thanks, Leon," J.C. said in his deep baritone. "First of all, let's set the record straight—if anyone's a superstar, it's Leon Bausch!" And with that he looked toward Leon and started to clap. The entire assembly joined in.

J.C. walked toward a flip chart and picked up a marker. "You should know that a flip chart and a marker are to a college professor what a hydrant is to a dog... just irresistible!"

Everyone laughed, especially Leon.

J.C. then talked about leadership. "For a minute, I want you to close your eyes." There was a low murmur in the crowd. J.C. waited. "OK, now I want you to think about the best boss or leader you ever had. Get that person's face in your head. Now, answer three simple questions: (1) How did this person make you feel? (2) What did she or he do that made you feel that way? and (3) What was your response to this person?"

The room went quiet. J.C. noticed smiles on many faces. It looked like the audience was having the same, very pleasant dream. Then he asked the crowd to open their eyes.

"OK. How did your favorite boss make you feel? Just toss out the words." He heard *Respected, Listened to, Heard, Safe, Worthy, Valued, Like I mattered, Important, and Smart.* J.C. recorded all the words on a flip chart.

"Thanks. So what did your boss do that made you feel that way?" The group accommodated. *Trusted me. Asked me my opinion. Treated me like an equal. Appreciated my thoughts and ideas.*

"Great. So how did you respond to that kind of treatment?" Once again the group was enthusiastic: *I'd do anything for her. I never wanted to let him down. I'd walk through a wall for her. I'd do whatever it took.*

"Final question : How do you all feel right now?" With no hesitation members of the group shouted out *Great, Happy, Thankful, Blessed, Lucky.*

J.C. explained that he'd done this exercise with FBI agents, prosecutors, engineers, lawyers, doctors, and any profession you could name, and the results are ALWAYS the same. In fact, he emphasized, we all know what good leadership looks like when we finally see it.

"On the other side of the coin," he explained, "we also know what it does NOT look like: autocratic, demeaning, insulting, short-tempered, impatient...and so on. But we often have experienced 'leadership' as a kind of command and control model. So, we pass on that learned leadership model when we become leaders—knowing full well it does not work."

"So, today, if I showed you a simple, easy-to-remember model of leadership that will give you the same kind of results your "Best Boss" gave you, would that be of interest to you?"

Everyone nodded as if in church and saying "Amen." And with that, J.C. drew the following diagram:

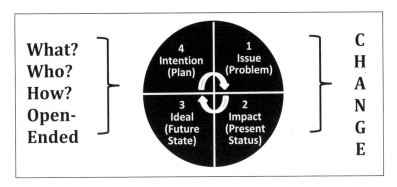

"Let's take an employee who comes to you with a problem—something she's having a tough time with," J.C. said. "However, rather than grab that sticky problem that will cling to you like Velcro, I'm going to ask you to develop very short arms. 'Alligator arms.'"

J.C. explained. Alligators have extremely short arms. Thus, when people come into the office and try to give their problem away, the "recipient" should think of the alligator with such short arms that it couldn't take the problem, even if it wanted to!

"Rather, use the coach-approach to help them solve their own issues," J.C. said.

He then explained that the key to great leadership was that no matter what the issue brought to you by colleagues, friends, family, or direct reports, the best approach was to ask four kinds of questions about four segments of the coaching clock related to solving any problem.

"I call it a 4x4 approach to leadership," J.C, said, "Here's the first 4—the four best questions to ask anyone if you're curious about solving any problem: What? Who? How? And Open-Ended questions.

He provided a couple of examples. One was about a friend who was thinking about buying a new car. "You might ask: What was the big issue pressing her to buy the car now?" he said. "What would the car be used for primarily? What or how was this impacting on her life?"

J.C. added that exploring the issue or problem with questions prevents people from pushing too fast toward solving the wrong problem! "That's where the second 4 in the 4x4 system comes in—the four segments of the coaching clock—enter into the equation," he said, pointing to the diagram. "And all these 4-I's: The Issue, Impact, Ideal, and Intention."

Then on cue, Margaret passed out a bright yellow sticky note to everyone and J.C. asked them to draw a miniature picture of the entire diagram on the sticky. He called it "The Magic Sticky Note." If they copied down the diagram he showed them today, practiced it daily for a month, they'd change their lives. He suggested sticking the note to their desktop and moving it daily—so it didn't just become background wallpaper—but something they actively noticed each day for one month—the time to create the neural pathways of a new habit.

He then began to explain the four segments of the coaching clock, saying how important it was to spend sufficient time on the first segment, "The Issue or Problem." Asking What, Who, How and Open-Ended questions to explore, uncover, and clarify the problem before trying to solve it isn't just smart business—it's critical to addressing the *real issue.*

"You don't want the perfect answer to the wrong issue; rather, a decent answer to the right one," J.C. said with a big smile. "Hey, I don't need to design a complex spaceship just to go to the grocery store!"

The crowd laughed. "Now let me tell you why it's called a coaching clock," J.C. said. He took it in four steps.

Step #1—The Issue: J.C. explained that whenever leaders have a finite and limited time to discuss issues, it was especially important that they spend a proportionate, even a disproportionate, amount of that time in the **Issue** segment of the clock. He said that most people typically spend only a few minutes deciding what the issue is and then jump right into problem solving, often with unsatisfactory outcomes.

"Look at some of the wars we've gotten ourselves in over faulty issue identification—Vietnam and Iraq come to mind. Doesn't matter if you're a Democrat or Republican—a rush to judgment after skipping over The Issue, takes you down a bad path with bad outcomes," he said.

Step #2—The Impact: Next, J.C. stated that people need to ask the same four What, Who, How and Open-Ended questions about *The Impact of the Present State* of the issue or problem. He showed them how to use numbers to help people give "valence" or degree of the impact.

"If you're trying to coach someone, you have to know how big the problem is," he said. "How's it affecting the person emotionally, financially, and other ways that have an impact on the person, unit, or company? Where does it stand as of today—right now?" Also, the person needs to consider the consequence of the present state. In other words, if nothing changes, what's the likely future?

"For example," he explained, "you might ask on a scale from 1 to 10 with 1 a low impact score and 10 the highest in your life, how would you rate this issue or problem?" If someone rated an issue an 8 or 9, then it was well worth taking time to address. However, if it were a 2 or 3, he challenged whether it was worth spending the time and energy.

Step #3—The Ideal State: "You have to have a target to hit one!" J.C. said. "Knowing the ideal, best possible state helps direct collective thinking toward the ideal end state—think of it as your vision of the ideal future."

J.C. was quick to explain that you're not guaranteed to hit the ideal state, but knowing what it is assures that you'll get reasonably close. Without such an ideal vision of best-possible state, you don't even have a prayer of getting there. What will be the alternative routes to get you there? What are the barriers that might inhibit you and what or who are the things and people who might help you reach The Ideal State?

Step #4—Intention: Then J.C. looked into the audience and paused for a moment. "To get anything in life done, you have to have intention," he said. "The equation is simple: no intent, no results. Intention is all about setting up a plan to get from the current Impact State to the Ideal State and making yourself accountable for the plan."

This was where the rubber met the road. Action is all that matters in this process. No action, no movement toward the solution. "So, if we come up with a great new product or solution, but no one is willing to take on the responsibility for making it happen, then nothing happens, and the status quo wins. Eventually, a competitor takes you on in your own backyard.

"Never underestimate the power of the status quo!" he said as he wrote the words on the flip chart and underlined them for emphasis. "That's it in a nutshell—a simple but amazingly effective way to problem solve," J.C. said, turning the microphone back over to Leon.

Leon cleared his throat and asked everyone to try this system for one month. "Try it at home, at work, at play," he said. "Use the sticky note as your reminder. Then, when someone presents a problem to you, I want you to take what I call a 'Coach-Approach for Leaders,'" he said, using his fingers to sketch quote marks in the air. Leon added that the leader's job was not to solve the issue or problem but to coach others to solve their own problems and to be accountable for following through.

"Walk that person through the 4x4 Coach-Approach process and see if it doesn't work every time. Speaking of time," Leon said looking at his watch, "I think it's time to eat." And right on cue, six waiters in tuxedos came in with shining silver platters of food and laid them on long tables they draped with white linen. In less than a minute, a banquet appeared. Everyone watched it evolve in amazement.

"So let's eat!" Leon said with gusto.

Sitting quietly in the back of the room, Margaret reviewed the brief notes she had taken as both J.C. and Leon had spoken:

The Coach-Approach to Leadership

- Ask, don't tell—LISTEN
- Four questions: What? Who? How? and Open-Ended
- The Coaching Clock:

- The Magic Sticky Note!

[55]

Chapter 3
The Lesson

Jake Diaz, VP for sales and marketing at Pacific, was 34 and a real charmer. With his short, sandy blond hair and blue eyes, he looked like a surfer, and he always made an entrance. As the head of business development, Jake was responsible for all government contracting and relationship building within government agencies—and he was very good at it. For the past several years Jake had not only hit his revenue numbers, he'd blown them out of the water. But something was going on lately, and he'd just gotten a note from Isaiah, the soft-spoken COO.

Isaiah Dove, a tall 42-year-old light-skinned African American with sharp angular features, possessed calmness akin to that of a Tibetan monk. At a trim and muscular 6'5" Isaiah towered over most everyone at Pacific, though he tried never to overshadow anyone, especially Leon, with whom he'd worked before Pacific and whom he loved like a father. As flashy and showy as Jake was, Isaiah was reserved and conservative.

When Jake entered Isaiah's office, he carried charts and graphs as well as a stack of papers. His all-cotton blue striped Ralph Lauren shirt sleeves were rolled up, and because the weather was sultry, as it typically was during summer in northern Virginia, he wasn't wearing his almost ever-present sport coat. "Hey, Isaiah, I think I can explain what's going on," he said. "This has been a crappy, and I mean crappy, quarter but I think we'll turn it around pronto. Here, let me show you." He rolled out the charts he'd brought, completely covering Isaiah's desk.

Isaiah gazed through his wire-rimmed glasses with some amusement at what was unfolding. He allowed Jake to work off his nervous energy for a bit and then said, "Jake, please sit down and relax."

"Relax," Jake said as if it were a new foreign word to him. "It's just that..." Isaiah motioned a calm gesture toward the big seat near the front of his desk. "Please, have a seat."

When Jake finally sat down, he did indeed relax.

Isaiah smiled and said, "You've done an extraordinary job for the company. I just wanted to call you in to thank you personally."

"Thank me... really?" Jake straightened up in his chair.

"Yes. From what I've seen reviewing the records, Pacific has become a major force in government contracting, largely because of the work you and your team have done over the past few years."

"Well, sure. Thanks for, well... thanking me and my team."

"I just want to know how I can help you going forward during this slump in the economy," Isaiah said.

"Hmm... I, ah. Well, I have some charts, here. But, you asked..."

"Look, I know there's not much you or I single-handedly can do to change the world economy. So, I guess my question is what issues or problems do you see in front of you that maybe we could tackle together?"

Jake thought a moment and then said, "Really, it's bandwidth."

"Can you explain that a bit for me? Tell me more...help me understand?" Isaiah asked with almost Buddha-like calmness and gentle smile.

"Sure. When the work is flowing, you're making lots of sales and showing up as a finalist in bids. In those times, sales and marketing is relatively easy. It's like fishing in a well-stocked pond."

Isaiah just nodded slightly. "OK."

"But when the pond gets fished out or they stop stocking it, it gets harder, much harder, to snag a fish. So, if you want to catch as many fish as you did before, you have to increase the number of people fishing."

"That makes sense," Isaiah said, nodding his head slowly.

"Problem is that the more anglers you have, the more expenses you incur."

[58]

"So, is the issue that you need more salespeople?"

"Yes and no."

"Can you explain?"

Jake told Isaiah that he did need a new augmented sales force, one that he might not keep beyond a year or so, but that he needed to get through these leaner times of low-stocked ponds. However, he was certain that Sandy Altman, the tough-fisted CFO, would deny it or at the very least use such an expense as a reason to criticize his department. He was concerned about the appearance of it but needed the help. He made all the points for increased marketing, advertising, and sales expense—more in a time of need than when all boats were floating on high tide.

"So, then the issue is more about how you will justify the expense to Sandy?"

"I suppose, yes."

"I don't hear real conviction in your voice."

So, Jake revealed that he'd never been comfortable around Sandy. She had a no-nonsense, stern, and almost hostile and judgmental way that made him nervous and less settled around her. Consequently, when he went in to brief her, things came out backwards and awkward.

"So, then could the real issue be your relationship with Sandy, especially during uncertain economic times?"

"Bingo! That's it."

"Can we explore the impact of the present state of your relationship with Sandy?" Isaiah asked.

Jake explained that ever since he'd come to Pacific, Sandy and he had never sung from the same sheet of music. She was all about the numbers; he and his team were all about customer relationships. She never smiled, either at him or at much of anything. So, he'd steered clear of her unless he absolutely needed to talk to her.

"On a scale from 1 to 10—where 1 is low and 10 is high—how would you rate your relationship with her?"

"A 6 maybe?"

"OK, and how important is it for you to have a strong relationship with her on the same 1 to 10 scale?

"A 9 or a 10!"

"OK. What would an ideal relationship with Sandy look like?"

"Hey, wait a minute. You're using that coach-approach stuff on me, aren't you?" Jake said. "The stuff that J.C. talked about. I just noticed."

Isaiah smiled and said, "I guess so. It's just a way for us to get to the bottom of something very important to you."

"Absolutely! I just noticed what you were doing. So, I'm cool. Where were we? Oh, yeah, the ideal relationship." Then Jake described a relationship where he and Sandy might regularly interact personally, casually and with some humor— not just in a serious, work-only, right-or-wrong way. That would start them off in any conversation in a friendly, open, and relaxed way—more ready to actually listen to each other.

At the prodding from Isaiah, Jake talked at length, describing very specifically what that situation might look like—such as going to lunch, catching coffee, maybe even having her go on a sales call or two with him—things like that. And when he'd finished, Jake seemed to feel better because he was now smiling.

"OK. So, going forward, I mean taking the first step, what's one thing you could do—just one easy step forward in that direction?" Isaiah asked.

Jake thought for a moment. "I'm not exactly sure."

"What if she were a new customer and you were trying to develop a relationship with her?"

"That's easy, I'd take her to lunch. Gives you time to talk, eat, and relax. I... wait a minute," he said, pausing. "Of course, I could just take her to lunch!" With that, a broad smile swept across Jake's face as he nodded his head responding to what he'd just said. "Yes, of course," he said more to himself than to Isaiah.

"That sounds like a start. When do you think you could do that?"

"I'm out of town next week, but could have it done in two weeks."

"Great, would you mind letting me know how it goes?"

"No problem. And, thanks, Isaiah."

After Jake left, Isaiah looked down at his own "magic sticky note" and smiled. He then made some notes on a piece of paper:

The Coach-Approach

- Who? What? How? Open-Ended?
- 4-I's—Issue, Impact, Ideal, Intention
- The "Issue" <u>is not</u> always the real issue!
- Follow up w/ Jake in two weeks.

About two weeks later, Isaiah and Jake were getting coffee at a local Starbucks. "So, Jake, how's it going?" Isaiah said.

"Very well, I must say. Sandy and I have been connecting more. I even had her come with me on a few big client calls."

"Really. How'd that go?"

Jake explained that before inviting Sandy to come along on his key account calls, he'd practiced "the Coach-Approach" with his friends, his direct reports, some clients, and just about anyone he could talk to. At first it was difficult not to just give answers or make conclusions, which were so natural for him. Slowing down to listen, think, and ask questions to better understand the problem was really hard.

"I'd ask a question, and if people weren't fast enough, I'd offer an answer to get them to speed things up. My impatience was my biggest barrier."

"Great observation. What else did you discover?"

"When I slow down—by asking questions—my judgment got better. I got better information to decide with. I especially got better with clients."

"How so?"

Jake explained that he's always sold the sizzle and not the steak. He loved showing clients all the bells and whistles of consulting services, "all the stuff we can do... a capabilities brain dump," he said. And along with that, he'd shown them long lists of impressive clients. Recently, Jake had noticed clients' eyes beginning to glaze over during his presentations. So, most recently he's started by identifying first what their biggest issue or problem was.

"So, how'd that work?"

"Great. After time and attention on the problem, we clarified what the real issue was. Then, I asked them about the impact of the current status. That made the problem come alive."

"How so?"

Jake explained that clients got more passionate when they realized how the issue or problem was affecting them and their company. Once he and the client understood the level of impact, the need to solve it became more important in the client's mind. Asking what the ideal state of this issue might look like for the client, presented the opportunity to sell, refer, or offer help.

"When clients listed several aspects of their ideal state," Jake explained, "I just would listen hard and either offer how one of our products might help solve this issue or refer them to a corporate partner. Or suggest whatever I could do to help them."

"Great."

"Then, I set up a follow-up meeting in a week or two, after I'd had time to research how I might help them. Sometimes I got the sale, sometimes, not. But every time I got goodwill working... and I'll start keeping track of how that pays off. I definitely enjoy the process better."

"What did Sandy say when she observed you in action?"

"We were at the Department of Justice," he began. Then he explained that they were working with the training and development department. A contact of Jake's had arranged for him to meet the Deputy AG for training, and Jake spent the entire meeting asking questions, which raised issues, sharpened the focus of the meeting, and created a lot of rapport.

"At the end of the meeting, the new Deputy said that he wanted a follow-up briefing of our consulting capabilities at their next retreat in a month, and asked if I could make it. Of course, I agreed."

After the meeting, Jake's contact told him how pleased he was, both for Jake and for himself.

"When Sandy and I got on the elevator, the first words out of her mouth were, 'Wow, I'm impressed!'"

"Me too," said Isaiah.

Chapter 4
The Crisis

Several months had gone by, and the leaves were beginning to turn colors. Things were moving along at a methodical pace that Leon liked to call his "ask and listen" stage. He'd been visiting with everyone in the company to learn what they did, what their opinions were, and what they most liked to do.

Then one afternoon, Jake Diaz called Margaret. "Tom Graff is at it again. He's going after every one of our clients—lowballing them with consulting fees below a hundred an hour. It's insane. Got calls from four clients last week and already three this week. Leon needs to be aware."

Margaret hung up the phone and told Leon, who didn't react. At first Margaret wasn't sure that Leon knew who Tom Graff was, so she began to explain. Leon politely stopped her. "I know Tom well—too well. He used to work for me. I fired him for lying on a proposal to one of our clients three years ago."

"Oh," Margaret said. Then she smiled and Leon returned the gesture. "Please get the executive team together today or first thing tomorrow so we can discuss a strategy for dealing with Tom."

At 8 a.m. the next day, the entire executive team gathered in the conference room.

Margaret was dressed in a simple but elegant sweater and tan slacks and her highlighted blond hair was brushed back away from her face. She sat next to Leon, who, as ever, wore his uniform of the day—a dark blue suit, white shirt, and striped red tie—dressed as if he were going to testify in court.

Jake Diaz, beaming in his starched open-necked blue cotton Polo shirt, rushed into the room and grabbed a chair at the end of the conference table. He tossed the light green linen sports jacket he'd been carrying on the chair next to him and rolled up his sleeves as he waited for the meeting to start.

Isaiah Dove sat next to Leon on the other side like a bookend to Margaret. Isaiah had worked for Leon before in two other companies. In fact, Leon had discovered him years ago working a menial job in one of Leon's previous companies. He'd helped Isaiah get his college education and eventually his MBA.

Sandy Altman sat next to Isaiah, and at six years with Pacific, was the longest-tenured person in the room and also the chief skeptic of the group. At 45 years old, she was short and stocky and dressed conservatively in dark slacks and starched white linen blouse with French cuffs and a simple gold chain around her neck. Her glasses and tightly pulled-back brown hair gave her a plain-Jane appearance, but she sported a tattoo on her left ankle of a Chinese symbol. Translated, it meant "Truth." But some employees took it to mean "No BS!"

Clara, Margaret's close friend and chief of administration, sat next to her. An attractive and fit former college soccer player, Clara's long black curly hair framed her attractive 33-year-old mocha-skinned face. A recent hire by Leon, Clara had worked for several companies, most recently, Tom Graff's company, Rock–Ledge Consulting, which she had left about six months before.

J.C. Williams, the executive coach, had become a regular at these gatherings, and he sat directly across from Leon. Clad in his usual blue blazer, starched shirt, and jeans, J.C. always looked like he was ready to start talking to Darden MBA students about leadership in the new economy and tough times.

Leon began the meeting by telling the story about Rock-Ledge and Tom Graff. He told about working with Tom for several years, described Tom's need to compete, and actually spoke highly of him, as was Leon's way about everyone. Then he explained about the contract that Tom inflated.

"I had warned Tom on two previous occasions when I had to retract untruthful claims that Tom had made about our experience and capabilities. After this, I realized that Tom was just wired differently than people I liked to work with. So we came to an agreement, and he left with a healthy severance and the best of luck. Needless to say, he wasn't happy. More like furious."

"No joke," Sandy said. "Recently, he's come after us on every contract we've competed for. He's like a stalking horse."

"More like a horse's—" Jake blurted, then stopped short. "He's killing us with his pricing. I don't know how he's making money at those rates."

"He's not," said Isaiah softly.

Everyone looked at each other in a kind of a frustrated realization that Isaiah was probably right.

Then, Leon spoke in words that sounded deliberate and measured. "Isaiah's correct. Tom just wants to take market share, and I suspect eventually ruin me. It's actually kind of a sad commentary about Tom." Leon told the group what he knew about Tom. He was competitive beyond normal; he not only loved to win, but he also hated to lose at anything. His termination by Leon for unethical conduct while an employee at Leon's former company had been the most difficult and humiliating failure Tom Graff had ever faced. His acrimony toward Leon went well beyond competition. And while Leon was not in any way scared of Tom Graff or his company, he thought that the Pacific executive team should focus on Graff as a serious corporate threat and solve this problem as a team.

"So, I've asked J.C. to guide us through this issue," Leon gesturing towards J.C. to take the helm.

J.C. sat up straight and leaned into the conference room table. "OK then, I'm going to ask you to join me in a short exercise that I call Leadership Flash team coaching—a kind of team problem solving when time and urgency are an issue." With that he flashed up on the screen in front of the group, the now familiar coaching process slide:

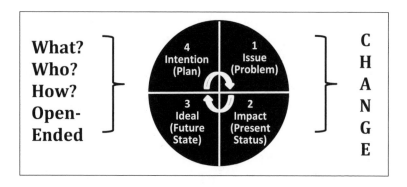

Rising from the table and moving toward the flip chart, J.C. told them that he would only ask them questions, the key simple ones that they were by now very familiar with— What? Who? How? and Open-Ended Questions—the very four questions he'd taught the group at the company gathering. He also explained the only two rules of this process after he wrote them on the flip chart:

1. People can only make statements in response to questions that anyone, including J.C., might ask.

2. As the coach, he had the right to ask questions, intervene, and discuss the process whenever necessary.

"We OK with the rules? Any questions?" He paused, waiting for their assent.

Everyone nodded. He flipped the chart to a blank page and printed in bold letters: "The Issue." Then he asked "OK...what exactly is the issue facing us?"

"Tom Graff's a jerk!" Jake said. The group chuckled.

"All right, so how is he a jerk?" J.C. asked. "What does he do?"

"He finds out which federal agencies we're targeting and then offers a price that he knows is WAY below market pricing. And then if he loses, he contests the bid...every time."

"And how does he find out who we're going after?" asked Isaiah.

Jake responded, "I don't know."

J.C. thanked Isaiah for the great question and reminded the group that anyone could ask anyone else a question... but no statements were to be made unless responding to a question—and that this was a technique used for getting to the heart of the issue quickly and with purpose.

Following that, J.C. and others asked and answered questions relentlessly. After a while, J.C. stopped the action and asked everyone at the table to take an index card and write down what they thought the real problem was. They all hit all around the issue—Tom Graff wanted to dominate the industry. Graff wanted to remove any competition by scooping up customers with an iron rake.

Next, J.C. read out their individual cards and inquired about the problem and asked the group—especially Leon—how close they were getting to the real problem. Leon leaned in and shrugged his shoulders.

So J.C. initiated another 15 minutes of discussion and had the group write out their impressions until Leon and the group finally agreed on the problem: Tom Graff's company was a real threat to Pacific because Graff's actions seemed targeted at hurting Leon and Pacific Consulting and not necessarily at winning new customers or market share.

Clara, the athlete of the group, said, "It's like he's playing in the Super Bowl but more interested in hurting our players than really winning the game."

"Good analogy," Jake said.

"OK," J.C. said. He turned to a fresh page and printed "Impact of Present State."

"So, let's move to step 2. What do you all see is the impact of the present state of this issue?"

Jake and Sandy shared their perspectives. Jake listed 10 customers that had been specifically targeted by Rock-Ledge, a company named for the risk-taking, mountain-climbing hobby of its owner, Tom Graff. Sandy noted that the financial impact up until now had been moderate but that the loss of the latest rounds of clients Rock-Ledge had taken away had begun to impact the annual revenue projections. "If he keeps pace, come mid-year, we'll be hurting puppies. What's more, his bid protests are costing us a lot in legal fees, let alone wasted time preparing for frivolous protests."

J.C. smiled and wrote down some of her more colorful words. "Anything else? Margaret, how about you?" he asked.

Margaret looked over at Leon and said that she felt that Tom Graff was personally out to hurt Leon—first and foremost—by hurting the company. She felt like Pacific was in the "crosshairs" of an assassin.

"I like the analogy. It helps us understand your honest emotional sense about what's going on. "Thanks, Margaret," J.C. said, then looked around for any hands in the air. The discussion went on for 10 more minutes.

Then J.C. flipped to the next clean page on the chart and printed "Ideal State."

"Let's go on to Step 3—What does the ideal state look like for this issue? If Pacific got tapped by a magic wand tonight and all were perfect tomorrow, what would it look like if the Rock-Ledge threat were gone... out of sight, and we had clear sailing?"

Throughout the animated discussion that followed, Leon sat, listened and made occasional notes.

Jake said that client retention would be back up to 90 percent "and our win rate of competitive proposals would exceed 75 percent."

"What else?" J.C. said, asking each person individually, as if they were in a focus group. The ideas flowed:

- The books would be solid black.
- No employee turnover.
- New opportunities would be coming in every day.
- Pacific would be going after proposals and contracts and winning most of them.

Then J.C. halted the discussion. "Isaiah, I noticed that you've been very quiet. I wanted to give you a chance to reflect."

Isaiah stroked his neatly trimmed goatee. "I wonder if this kind of competition is ultimately healthy for our company."

"Healthy! Are you nuts?" Jake said.

J.C. put up his hand like a traffic cop. "Jake, exactly what question are you answering?"

"It's just that..."

"Remember the rules... answers only follow questions. No pronouncements or speeches. OK, Isaiah, continue your response to my question, please," J.C. said to get the train back on the track.

Isaiah said that Pacific had gotten fat and happy and sales effort had become lazy.

Jake turned beet red and summoned all his will power to shut up. But it looked like he would blow any minute.

"We let Graff sneak up on us because we were asleep at the switch. We were taking orders but not selling," Isaiah continued. "Look, I'm NOT just talking about marketing but ALL of us got comfortable—me included. Now I feel like we're finally getting our heads out of the sand."

J. C. wrote notes on the chart as Isaiah spoke.

Then J.C. spoke again. "O.K. How about Step 4? What's our intention as a team going forward? How do we get from our present state to the ideal state? What should we stop doing or start doing?" Again, he decided to be inclusive by asking each participant to respond.

Lots of discussion emerged. As J.C. brought the meeting to a close, he asked what everyone could contribute before the group met again on this issue. Essentially, the team members agreed to take on assignments.

- Jake would formulate a new sales counter-attack.

- Sandy would project figures for the rest of the year.

- Margaret would help by calling key accounts.

- Isaiah volunteered to monitor operations and determine any ways that Graff might be finding out what accounts Pacific was pursuing.

"And I will meet with Tom face to face," Leon said matter-of-factly.

As usual, Jake blurted out what everyone else was thinking. "What!!"

Clara pushed back her black curly hair and addressed Leon. "I think I can help with background information before you meet with Tom. I have a pretty good sense for his state of mind, having just left Rock-Ledge."

"First, I'll keep operations stable," Leon quietly responded, "and second, I will be happy to help anyone get the needed information as quickly as possible."

"Thanks," J.C. said, "Right, let's not forget to keep the regular trains running, as we plan how to lay track on a new route."

Finally, Leon said almost matter-of-factly, "I'll schedule my face-to-face discussion with Tom... this week."

After the meeting, Margaret made some notes to help her with the process she'd just learned:

Leadership Flash Team Coaching

1. People can only make statements in response to questions. Anyone can ask anyone else a question.

2. The coach had the right to ask a question, intervene, and discuss the process whenever necessary.

3. 4-I's: Issue – Impact – Ideal – Intention

4. Questions: Who? What? How? Open-ended?

Chapter 5
The Meeting

A few days before Thanksgiving, Leon sat in Rock-Ledge Consulting's stark black-and-white waiting room. After an intrusive buzz to the front desk, he was escorted into the expansive office of Tom Graff, who did not get up when Leon entered, desperately trying not to drag his right leg and look weak.

"Leon, sit down," he said, never extending his hand. "What happened to your leg?"

"Age," he said with a wry half-smile, while easing himself into the chair without showing weakness.

"OK, so what brings you here today?" Graff added, lacing his hands behind his head as if settling back for a casual conversation with a subordinate.

"One of the reasons I wanted to talk to you is about all of your bid protests and sniping of our clients."

Graff bristled. "What's the matter Leon, afraid of some competition?"

The two went back and forth about their corporate competition and ethics. Leon expressed his regret at the way things had ended for Tom when Leon had to let him go.

"Great time to raise that, Leon, now that you're getting your butt kicked. How's it feel?" Graff said staring right through Leon.

"Look, I came here to settle any animosity between us, and allow our two companies to fight it out fairly in the marketplace," Leon said, "without the any behind-the-scenes baggage between you and me. So, Tom, how can I set our relationship straight?"

"You can't! That's why I took the meeting today. I wanted to tell you face to face that I'm not stopping until I pay you back for the humility you caused me and my family. This IS personal AND professional, Leon. So, deal with it." By now, Graff sat forward, palms on his desk as if he were a panther about to pounce.

"I'm sorry to hear that, Tom, and hope that you might reconsider your position."

"I won't. I've said what I wanted to. Now I'll ask you to leave, Leon."

With some effort, Leon stood up and stuck out his hand to shake and say goodbye. Graff just looked at Leon's hand, then looked him in the eye, and shook his head

Later that same evening, Leon sat in his chair while his dog, Roscoe, sat on the floor beside him. An Australian cattle dog, Roscoe was always dragging a sock or a ball for Leon to toss so he could retrieve it. Leon tossed the sock across the room a few times, but Roscoe was so fast at retrieval that finally Leon said, "That's it for tonight, boy. I'm tired."

Roscoe looked up at Leon, as if waiting for Leon to say more. "Roscoe, I miss Emma," Leon said, reminiscing about his deceased wife of 45 years. And with that Leon launched a conversation with Roscoe and Emma as if she were there sitting on the couch in her favorite seat. He told Emma how much he missed her as he wiped a tear from his cheek. Then he apologized to Roscoe about being so emotional. Roscoe seemed to understand—he tilted his head to the side like a comforting friend.

"Sometimes I wonder why I bought Pacific. What was I trying to prove—that I could do it again—that I still had the right stuff?"

Leon pushed his hands through the white wisps of hair on his balding head. Finally, he pulled them over his eyes, as if he wanted to catch his breath and refresh his thoughts.

"Roscoe, if Emma were here, she'd put her hand on my shoulders and tell me everything will turn out fine. She'd say, 'Leon, it's not a perfect world, sweetie.'"

Then Leon pulled the framed picture of Emma off the nearby coffee table and spoke to her picture directly. "I miss you, honey. I miss you so, so much."

Chapter 6
The Announcement

The Wednesday after Thanksgiving, the six executive team members and J.C. again gathered around the conference room table at Pacific Consulting. Leon thanked everyone for being there and turned the meeting over to J.C.

"OK, let's start this session of leadership flash team coaching with updates. What did everyone do?"

Jake described a new aggressive plan that his business development team would launch in two weeks. They would focus on growing the revenues by 20 percent by the end of the year. It would require investing in technology, process, and people and would be significant. Looking at Leon, he said, "The level of competition that we will bring to the market might invite more robust challenges from Tom Graff."

Leon just smiled faintly and nodded.

Sandy passed out a series of spreadsheets that she also flashed up on the screen at the front of the conference room. With great detail and clarity, she demonstrated that if even half of Jake's projections came through, the company would experience a 22 percent revenue bump with net up almost 3 percent. She never smiled much except to say, "You all know that my nature is a bit more conservative." Jake wasn't sure whether to smile or frown, so, he just smiled.

Margaret reported that she, after consulting with Jake, had called their key accounts as a courtesy to survey their needs. She had acted as an honest broker for the firm by collecting data on how happy they were with the service. What did people think the firm did well and what could the firm improve on?

"And, I'm happy to report that there's a high satisfaction level among all of our top 30 accounts," she said. "Really, it's remarkable. I have the specifics, but over a 90 percent positive rating in the top three categories... quality, service, and responsiveness."

"Thanks, Margaret. "How about you, Clara?" J.C. asked. Clara passed out a three-page backgrounder titled, "Rock-Ledge Consulting." "Let me give you a top-level preview of this report," Clara said. "Rock-Ledge is aggressive and well-funded, but reckless. Tom Graff's personality is bold, risk-taking, and belligerent. He's fueled more by anger and competition than by strategy. Ironically, that anger motivates him and at the same time is his vulnerability."

"Huh?" Jake asserted to the amusement of all because he usually reflected the collective emotion of the group.

Clara explained that Graff had made several bold moves when angry and had gotten several big hits. On the other hand, he'd had some real catastrophes, such as when he'd gone head to head with another stubborn, better-funded, and more strategic firm. They'd "cleaned his clock." In anger he sued them, and they counter-sued. And Graff lost big.

J.C. nodded, "Very interesting indeed. Thanks, Clara. Isaiah, anything interesting come up from your review?"

Isaiah lifted his head and wryly smiled. "Just another day in paradise."

The group smiled and chuckled.

"Seriously, I've found operations to be chugging along without much of a hitch. Also, I haven't found much about how Graff's anticipating our targets, but I'd caution everyone here and your staffs to limit conversations about our marketing activities outside the office."

"Thanks, Isaiah. Leon, do you want to tell the group how your meeting with Graff went?"

"Well, right before the holiday, I visited Tom... let's just say it was not a love fest."

Everyone laughed. Leon explained the gist of the meeting. "In essence, Tom has declared corporate war."

Leon thanked the team for the fire-drill responses to J.C.'s leadership flash team coaching—especially with such flash-point issues. Then he said, "And while fighting a war is the least productive way to become more profitable, we'll have to prepare—but we have to be smart, not reactive—strategic, not just tactical."

He explained that the next phase of planning and team decision making would shift to being more methodical, strategic, and slower... but ultimately more thoughtful. J.C. would introduce the more strategic Leadership Action Learning approach at another meeting in the very near future.

Then, Leon cleared his throat and abruptly changed topics. "Over Thanksgiving, I decided to give away the company."

There was a kind of collective gasp as he let the idea seep in. Then he explained the details. First, he told the group that he had always wanted his employees to have a stake in his company. His lawyer had told him about the ESOP program.

"You mean like the fables... Aesop's fables?" Jake interjected.

Leon laughed. "Not quite, Jake. An ESOP is an Employee Share Option Plan." He passed around a copy of an explanation about the ESOP. "Basically, I'm going to give the ownership of the company to everyone who works here."

Clara asked, "What are the implications?"

"On a day-to-day basis, not much. I'll still be the CEO, and you all will be the executive leadership."

He further explained that when the company's fully owned by employees, they act as the shareholders and owners. In essence, *all* employees, including executives and line workers, would collectively have the capacity to influence what Pacific does or does not do, as do any stockholders of a publicly traded company. They get to vote thumbs up or down on the annual budget, strategic direction, and on who runs the show.

"It can be a little complicated, but in essence, it's a good deal for employees and all of you in this room, especially if we continue to do what we're good at and stick to our strategy."

"What's the down side?" asked Jake.

Sandy spoke up, "Employees get a bigger say in how the company gets run. Sometimes that can lead to issues of control and definition of who gets that control and how they get to do that."

Leon stepped in, "Look, I've set up more than a couple of ESOPs in my life for clients and know the territory well. All I ask is that you trust that I know how to do this in gradual steps, which I'll explain fully to you first and then to employees. But as I said, in the final analysis, any number of our employees and you here in this room might become financially well off."

Leon gave his executive team time to read the document, then said, "Look, the bottom line is that the employees will have a stake in the company. I'll be distributing the stock so that each one of you will have a substantial equity base in the company, and if you stick around for five years, you'll all do very well, along with all the employees.

Sandy Altman, the CFO, spoke up: "Leon, that's extraordinarily generous. Are you sure about this?"

"Absolutely."

The rest of the team sat stunned and just kept re-reading the document.

Margaret asked, "But doesn't that mean you, yourself, are giving up a lot of equity and control?"

"Yes."

"May I ask why you're doing that? I'm just trying to understand this," Margaret said slowly.

"As you can see, I'm not a young man," Leon smiled, "So, the best I can do is give back."

"Give back?"

"Look, I've been both lucky and fortunate. I've made a fair amount of... well let's just say, financially things have worked out well," Leon explained. "But to me life is like monopoly. You get to play it, buy properties, businesses, have ups and downs... but eventually you have to put all the money back in the box with all the pieces, so that in the future, after you're gone, someone else gets a turn to play. No one really owns the pieces. We just use them and then put them back in the box. That's what I'm doing, putting pieces and money back in the box."

"Thank you," Margaret said softly, smiling. "Thank you very much."

Leon nodded.

Sandy perked up. "THANK you!"

"Yes, Leon, thank you, I guess," Jake blurted, "....as soon as I understand it!"

Everyone laughed, especially Leon. Then the meeting broke up, leaving only Leon and Margaret at the table. Margaret started gathering her papers and getting up to leave. Leon said, "Can you stay for a few more minutes to chat, Margaret?"

"Of course," she said, and sat back down.

"You know how much I care for all you do for me."

Margaret blushed.

Leon explained that he was going to need more help, especially getting the ESOP up and running, and that he needed more support. So, if she were willing, he wanted to make Margaret a corporate officer, and his Chief of Staff.

"Chief of Staff? What does that mean?"

Leon explained that he wanted someone to coordinate the efforts associated with changing to the ESOP and to balance all the strong personalities of the executive team as they navigated this change and the others to come. He told her that he'd already spoken to the COO, Isaiah, and that between her and Isaiah, they'd keep the wheels rolling and people communicating with each other.

"And Isaiah agreed to that?"

"Enthusiastically. He's a quiet guy and can use your more gregarious, social touch to balance him during the upcoming changing times. He's going to have a lot going on next year."

"Well, I don't really know what to say," she said, looking directly into his eyes and shrugging her shoulders.

"A 'yes' would work for me," Leon said with a big smile. "And it means a substantial raise, too."

"Thank you so much. I'm just in a state of shock."

Leon smiled and asked her for a hand getting up from the chair.

[79]

When he got to his feet, he saw that Margaret had tears in her eyes; so, he lightly touched her shoulder.

"I was hoping this would be a happy day,'" Leon said.

"Oh, it is. Most definitely. It's just that now I can afford to get my mother better assisted living."

Leon did not know too much about Margaret's mother, only that she had some "health issues."

"May I ask about her health?" Leon said so formally that even he felt awkward.

"Of course. Mom's 75 and has early-onset Alzheimer's."

At first Leon just seemed to freeze in place, much as if he were posing for an artist.

"Leon, everything OK?" Margaret asked.

"Yes." He paused, trying to decide how much to reveal. "My late wife, Emma, eventually died from complications associated with Alzheimer's. So, I'm very familiar with that cruel disease."

"Sorry about your wife. Mom's still very functional, but I really want her in an assisted living place. Sometimes she forgets stuff—like forgetting to turn off the burner on the stove."

"How well I know. One day, I'd enjoy meeting your mother," Leon said.

Margaret hesitated for just a second. "Turns out I'm having dinner with her next week. Would love it if you could make it."

"Great," he said, smiling "Can't say no to my new Chief of Staff."

News of the ESOP spread quickly and everyone in the entire company soon became quite expert on what it meant to be an employee stockholder. And while the normal questions arose, Leon had scheduled regular briefings, set up an intranet website for questions and answers, and made the entire process transparent.

News of Margaret's promotion spread just as quickly and was universally accepted, especially among the executive leadership—all of whom saw her as the one who kept Leon and the group moving together as a team.

Chapter 7
The First Test

The certified letter came in the next morning's mail. Margaret opened the letter and brought it to Leon. He knew from her deep frown that the news wasn't good.

"It's a bid protest. Tom Graff lodged it over the Treasury consulting job," she said.

"I see. That's too bad."

"Won't that delay the contract award?"

"Yes."

Margaret hesitated and then asked, "Will that mean laying off people?"

"No. That's not happening as long as I'm running this company," Leon said with as serious a look as she'd ever seen him have.

"Great. Good to know because I just bought a new condo."

"I'm going to ask J.C. to meet with us today. If he's available, I'd like you to please get the executive team in the conference room a few minutes before his arrival."

At 2:00 p.m., the entire executive team sat around the conference room table at Pacific Consulting. Before Leon spoke, Margaret passed out a copy of the bid protest to everyone. Then, Leon opened the meeting.

"Thank you all for coming without much notice," he said. "I wanted you all to know about the bid protest and my philosophy about such bumps in the road."

Leon explained that he'd been through many government bid protests in his life both when he had owned companies and as inside corporate counsel. "They're annoying and generally a waste of time and money, but they're just part of the not-much-fun-stuff of doing business with the government, like paying taxes." Everyone chuckled.

"But more to my point: When such things occur, my philosophy is to treat them like temporary annoyances, which we can learn from but should never dwell on. So, no layoffs, no finger pointing, or any of that sort of stuff. As you all know, Tom Graff and I have a history, which I'm sure contributed to this aggressive behavior. Tom likes to win, especially if I'm on the opposite team." Everyone in the group broke into a smile.

Leon said he wanted to talk about more important issues than the bid protest: He wanted to revisit the direction of the company—to use this protest as a catalyst to focus the team on the future of Pacific. He wanted the team to start thinking strategically. But to do that, he said, he wanted to use a process called the Leadership Action Learning (LAL) team coaching process for decision making. He wanted to try it out today.

"I've asked J.C. to help us move to the next level—to help us develop a strategy moving forward. So, J.C., thanks for being here today on such short notice," Leon said, motioning to J.C., who was sitting next to him.

"Thanks, Leon."

First off, J.C. explained that they had already practiced a version of the LAL team coaching process when they did Leadership Flash team coaching to address the Tom Graff issue—and when they'd witnessed the coaching model he'd demonstrated when Leon took over the company. "It's all related," J.C. said. "So, this will just be a refinement of the process.

"OK, let me give you the Twitter version of Action Learning, the basis for what I call Leadership Action Learning team coaching for decision making," he said, smiling. "Action Learning at its heart is a question-focused group process that helps teams solve important business problems and become even better leaders in the process."

"Huh?" Jake said and shrugged his shoulders.

"Sorry. Let me give you some background."

J.C. explained that action learning was a process conceived by a Reg Ravens in the 1940s. Ravens worked at the Cavendish Labs at Cambridge University (England) with a number of Nobel laureates and was very impressed as he watched these big-brained physicists deal with each other in such respectful, productive ways. They solved complex problems largely by asking questions. In essence, their questions caused them to search for answers that led to deeper questions, answers, and ultimately, learning. Thus, was born the idea of action learning—that people learn best from asking and responding to honest, thoughtful, and respectful questions. In fact, we ask questions all the time, every day. What's the temperature outside? This question prompts us to check the thermometer and decide to wear a heavy coat or not. What does my new boss like or dislike? This question prompts us to observe, collect data, and make judgments that can be developed into an operational theory about how to best work with the new boss.

Then J.C. paused for dramatic effect.

"It must work!" he said. "Cavendish Labs produced 29 Nobel Prize winners! It's a process of asking questions, not giving answers—a simple but powerful method to solve big, complex problems that might have a number of possible paths to a solution."

J.C. explained that the process was both simple and powerful but initially counterintuitive to the way most people act.

"Without going too far into academic theory, let's just say your brain mostly operates using two systems. System 1 is the quick, unconscious function that makes thousands upon thousands of fast, unconscious decisions a day. Most of the time they're good ones, but sometimes not so much!" he said. Then he told the group that when the fast-thinking brain gets out of its area of expertise—into foreign territory but still moving fast—it's subject to errors, some of which can be damaging.

The other system at work in the brain is System 2—the slower, more deliberate conscious brain that acts as the brain's safety check... like a comptroller. Because it's slower and more deliberate, it can think through consequences and make better decisions. But it gets tired being bombarded by System 1 and often gives in like a tired father or mother who says "Yes" to a nagging child when he or she knows better.

Successful companies monitor System 1 thinking, especially when the territory is new and uncharted. They develop "yellow, slow-down lights" such as policies, oversight, and checklists—all of which keep the flood of intuitive decisions from overwhelming good judgment, especially when big stuff is at stake. On the other hand, people aren't as good at monitoring System 1.

Leadership Action Learning (LAL) provides teams and organizations with an important "yellow, slow-down light" *to ensure deliberative, diverse, and rational thinking—especially when the issues are very important but not urgent.* In other words, when considering big ideas—longer-term, strategic policy and practice guidance—LAL is a home run for at least two reasons. First, the process forces deliberation. Second, people learn many of the most important elements of leadership—listening, respect, asking questions, humility, and all that comes from slowing down and considering the diverse opinions of others.

"So let me explain just how this Leadership Action Learning works," J.C. said, moving to the flip chart. He explained each of the statements printed on each page, as follows:

1. Leon is the "problem presenter"

    a. Will take only a few minutes to express the problem or issue.

    b. The group asks questions to clarify the problem.

2. The team will use the Leadership Action Learning (LAL) team coaching process to help solve the problem.

   a. J.C. will be in charge of the coaching process, NOT the content.

   b. The team will be in charge of the content. They are EXPERTS and know MUCH more about Pacific Consulting than anyone else.

3. All persons in the group should stay open to what they might "learn" about being a good leader

   a. LAL (asking questions) slows down our thinking—saves us from jumping to rapid, faulty conclusions. LAL produces deliberate, diverse, and rational thought.

   b. Action Learning teaches a lot of leadership traits, such as how to speak with courtesy, how to listen, and how to be respectful—the BIG leadership traits.

   c. Such learning is critical to leadership development—as good as any MBA program could even hope to be.

4. The BIG Rules

   a. No one makes a statement, except in answer to a direct question.

   b. Anyone can ask anyone else—including the entire group—a question.

   c. As the "coach," J. C. will stop the proceedings to enhance learning or comment on the process.

When he finished his orientation, everyone nodded, signaling that they understood. So J.C. said, "OK, Leon, do you want to take no more than two to three minutes and tell us what you see as the big issue or problem you'd like to address?"

Leon proceeded to describe what he saw as the big, long-term issue facing the company. He spoke specifically about Pacific not having as clear a strategy. He'd read all the business intelligence he could about the company but still was not sure where the company was headed, which, ironically, was precisely why he bought it when he did. He thought that the company needed more clarity around its strategy and vision, for starters.

With that, J.C. sketched the "Coach-Approach Process" on the flip chart.

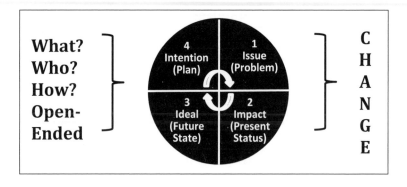

"You've seen this graphic before—when I spoke at the company gathering and when we used it for the Leadership Flash team coaching issue involving Tom Graff. We'll use it now to help understand the problem that Leon raised: Strategy," J.C. said. "Remember the key questions—What, Who, How, and Open-Ended Questions and the Four I's—and understand that we're in the Issue (problem) quadrant to start with. Let's stay in that quadrant until we know what the real issue is. And I'll let you know when that seems to be right. OK, so who has the first question for Leon?"

Naturally, Jake raised his hand first and said, "Have you thought about just looking at other company websites for strategy ideas?"

As he had promised in the opening instructions, when something required his comment around process, J.C. leaned in and stopped the action: "Jake, how can you ask that question so it's not so directive or leading?"

"Directive? But it's just a question."

"Try it another way, without trying to tell Leon what you think he should do—disguised as a question. Use one of the key questions we talked about, maybe?"

"OK. How might comparing similar corporate mission statements help the process?"

"Better," J.C. said, resisting the temptation to object at the veiled disguise of a leading question. Rather, he leaned back into his chair signaling the group to proceed.

Leon answered that he had looked at other websites but continued to look for benchmarking sites.

"Leon, what's your experience with vision statements?" Margaret asked.

"I like them if they're based on reality... part of the everyday culture, not something to be framed in a conference room for the Board of Directors to admire." Then, he explained that at a previous company, they had slogans all over the place. They began to seem like background, like wallpaper, such that no one even noticed them anymore. They became invisible. He wanted something different for Pacific—a strategy and vision that were living, real, and attainable—or at least approachable.

The discussion continued. After about 15 minutes, J.C. leaned in and interrupted. "OK, a couple of observations. First, I noticed that neither Clara nor Isaiah has yet to ask a question. So, I'll take the time to ask if either of you would like to ask one now or just 'pass.'"

Clara spoke first, "I'm fine with the direction of the conversation... no need to ask anything at this point."

"OK, fair enough. How about you, Isaiah?"

Isaiah just sat there for a few seconds, though it felt like much longer. "OK, I do have a question for Leon: What glimpses of the future do you see for Pacific?"

"Great question, Isaiah!" Leon said. Then he leaned back in his chair, thought for a moment and said, "I see Pacific Consulting bringing calm and clarity to our clients. Like a trusted friend might."

"OK. So, you do have a vision that helps us become a trusted friend?" Isaiah said.

"Sort of, but I'm not quite sure yet."

"Then what do you want us to do?"

"I guess I'd like you to consider that future state vision and/or help me clarify it."

Isaiah nodded "OK."

J.C. leaned forward. "Thanks, Isaiah, for helping solidify our thinking," he said. "Now, everyone take out a piece of paper and write down what you think the problem is."

After five minutes, J.C. asked people to read only what they had written. Responses varied:

1. Leon wants us to come up with his vision.

2. Leon wants input on a strategy and vision for the company.

3. Leon's confused and wants direction.

The list went on.

"OK. So, what themes are emerging?" J.C. asked.

Responses fell into a few categories: Leon wants to develop a strategy and a vision. The group sounded uncertain and confused. So, J.C. put the group back into session to focus on the question again.

After another 10 minutes of more productive questions and answers, J.C. stopped the process again and asked the group to write down what they now thought the problem was and to print their responses on yellow sticky notes, which he posted on the chart and numbered:

1. Leon has great hopes for Pacific and wants us all to come up with an ideal future vision and a path toward it—a new strategy.

2. Leon cares about the future of Pacific.

3. We need a vision or we'll never play with the big boys.

4. The vision has something to do with clarity for clients as well as clarity for our own team.

5. How do we help others see their vision and strategy for a better future, if we don't have our own strategy?

After filling up another flip chart page, J.C. asked Leon how these resonated with him.

"They're all very good. But today, I have to say that number 5 hits the closest to what I'm feeling. How do we do our job for our clients—help them with consulting strategy, vision and clarity—when we can't do it for ourselves? Yes, I think that's the big issue for me."

J.C. asked permission, and got it from Leon and the group, to move forward to Step 2, describing the Impact Quadrant—how the present or current status of Pacific's lack of strategy could impact its future.

Again, Jake was the first to respond after he pulled out a card from his wallet. "Here's what our current vision-values statement says: 'Pacific Consulting aspires to be the best-in-class consultant to our clients and become partners in our clients' success journey."

J.C. noted that Jake made a comment and did not pose a question. So he asked the group if someone would want to start the first question, perhaps around what Jake had just read to the group.

Margaret asked: "Jake, what does all that mean for us and our clients?"

"Do the best we can to help them get where they want to go—I guess."

From that point forward and for the next 30 minutes great, and at times heated, discussion ensued around what Pacific's current strategic vision statement really meant. Everyone agreed that the statement was about "the current state," but so vague as to be almost useless. After about 20 minutes of discussion everyone realized a few things: The mission statement sounded good but was fluff, no one could repeat it from memory, and it had no real impact on daily operations.

"OK," asked Isaiah. "So, how does this vision statement impact the company?"

"I think it hurts us competitively," Jake said.

Clara, who had been quiet until then, asked the group, "How have we quantified our vision?"

"We haven't," said Margaret, "Not that I'm aware of, at least."

The questions flowed freely at that point. When did the company ever have a strategic vision? What did the employees think about vision and strategy? How were stakeholders like customers and vendors brought in to help define the vision? What are the professional, emotional, and financial impacts of not having a clear vision? What are the barriers? What's the cost of not doing anything—the status quo?

The answers brought a starker reality to the discussion.

- The company had always had some sort of "token" strategy... but nothing with a heart or real passion.

- The employees were rarely ever consulted. Almost always, strategy was developed by the most senior executives working with a consultant.

- Stakeholders were never consulted either.

- The impact was inhibiting and even crippling at times.

- The company seemed rudderless and had for years.

When the discussion waned and not much more was forthcoming, J.C. said, "Excellent discussion. So, now that we have somewhat of a handle on the impact of the present state of Pacific's strategic issue, can we shift and talk about the ideal state?

Everyone nodded.

"OK, then, what would it look like if Pacific had a powerful, ideal vision statement and strategy focused on the company's primary intent?"

The discussion became energetic with people asking questions like these: What do we want to become? What do we want to discover along the way? What do we want to change?

After some time going back and forth, Isaiah summarized and put a punctuation mark on the discussion: "It seems to me that what we're saying is that we want ideally to build Pacific into the kind of government contracting company that government agencies want to work with and that great employees want to work for."

In the next 45 minutes, these points were made about the ideal state for vision and strategy at Pacific:

- We'd be better in tune with our customers, stakeholders, and employees.

- We'd be better able to help our own clients find their direction.

- We'd have a clear vision of who our best clients were.

- We'd be viewed as a better management team to our internal clients and strategic partners.

- People would never want to leave the company, and we'd have a long line of folks wanting to come aboard.

J.C. cleared his throat. "Let's move to another topic concerning the ideal state. I'd like us to do all do some systems thinking. By that I mean think about how we fit in context with the business ecosystem that Pacific is part of."

Clara asked, "What exactly is a business ecosystem?"

J.C. smiled and explained, but remained ever careful never to engage in the content discussion. He reminded the group that he would be in charge of the process—the content was their job. However, he offered that one possible approach to consider is SWOT—which he wrote on the flip chart.

"You may wish—as a process—consider the company's *internal Strengths and Weaknesses* as well as their *external Opportunities and Threats*—as just one standard, but certainly not the only way to approach strategy," J.C. said.

Sandy Altman, the steely-eyed CFO, spoke. "Internally, we've got strong employee loyalty and decent current technical strength," she said. "From a weakness perspective, we don't have the kind of bench strength we should have in systems engineering and cloud computing."

That launched a host of ideas that J.C. put up in a 2x2 matrix:

INTERNAL	EXTERNAL
Strengths: loyal employees, technical strengths, client base...	Opportunities:
Weaknesses: lack bench in systems engineering, cloud computing...	Threats:

Clara asked J.C. to clarify what "external opportunities and threats" meant. The external environment, he explained, included the economy, world events, government activity, and things that the company had no control over, but could likely be affected by any of them.

The list of external threats began to flow: The economy's hurting, the Middle East is unstable, and that means oil is up for grabs, Islamic radicalism was taking root in many poor countries and even having deep effects in long-term partners like Saudi Arabia and Egypt, and even less friendly places like Syria and Libya, where radical government changes were leading to certain instability.

Then, Isaiah asked "OK. Given these threats, how can Pacific optimize them?"

"Optimize?" asked Jake.

"Take advantage... get the most out of what might at first look like difficult situations."

That's when Sandy said, "Well, we're a virtual organization. So business disruption is a non-issue."

Other questions and answers developed: Pacific was free from oil costs... many folks worked virtually; they were able to take clients from around the world and not restricted to local markets.

When they'd finished, J.C. had made more notes on the SWOT chart:

INTERNAL	EXTERNAL
Strengths: loyal employees, technical strengths, client base...	Opportunities: virtual company, national and international capacity, flexibility, speed...
Weaknesses: lack bench in systems engineering, cloud computing...	Threats: costs could rise, uncertainty might slow business, fear could paralyze...

And when it came to the discussion of stakeholders, the group named many: employees, their families, owners, investors, senior leaders, people on the way up, new hires, future hires, competitors, teaming partners, the local business community, and more. It seemed as soon as one stakeholder was named, two more seemed to pop up.

"Stakeholders are everywhere, when you just stop and think about it!" Jake said with a straight face. Everyone cracked up as did he, once he'd taken the time to think about what he'd said. "Duh!"

J.C. looked at the faces of the team and then at his watch. "I'm sensing that we're about fried and need to call it a day," he said. "So, let's move toward the Intention Quadrant—planning and accountability. We're scheduled to meet every two weeks for a couple of hours. So that means between then and now, each of you needs to do some work. So, who's willing to do what before we meet again?"

Sandy Altman agreed to work on the SWOT matrix and to flesh out a list of key stakeholders. She said she would use "Survey Monkey" to get information from staff.

Isaiah said that he would take charge of understanding the strategic thoughts and intentions of key stakeholders. He'd have extended talks with everyone in the room, develop an anonymous survey, talk to key investors, and customers—in other words, take the temperature of the key stakeholders. So, he'd work closely with Sandy as she developed her list of stakeholders.

Clara volunteered to think about what expansion and new directions would mean to the support systems—like information technology, purchasing, accounting, and all the systems to support any new strategic intent.

Jake said his head hurt and that he would take some Tylenol® before the next meeting! Everyone laughed. Then, he agreed to look at the entire marketing effort and what kind of a system retooling it would take for them to scale up the model for future expansion and sophistication.

Margaret said that she would do an extensive review of all the historical data about the company and of all the contracts they'd won and lost—and any useful intelligence she could glean from that analysis.

Leon then worked his way up toward the front of the room. He cleared his throat and said, "First, let me thank J.C. for his very elegant handling of such a rowdy crowd!" He smiled and winked. "I also want to thank you all as you formulate the future of Pacific. My main job for the next meeting is to stay out of your way!"

J.C. stepped forward and said, "Thanks to you, Leon, for your kind words. And thanks to you all for being such great participants in the process today. So what did you learn today that might help you as leaders? Leon, how about you?"

"I learned that the problem is not always the first thing that pops into your head," Leon responded.

Jake said, "I learned how hard it is to ask questions and really listen."

Margaret said, "I learned how powerful questions stopped and made people think."

Sandy said, "It helped me be more curious and patient... which I need at home as well as at work!"

Clara said, "I agree with what everyone else has said."

Jake blurted out, "Come on, Clara... how about you?"

Clara said, "I learned that I really can contribute to the discussion."

Finally, Isaiah said, "I learned that my basic nature fits this process well, and that makes me feel good."

J.C. thanked everyone again and reminded them to come back in two weeks with their updates.

When he'd finished, Margaret took a couple of minutes to sketch out her notes about today's meeting:

Leadership Action Learning (LAL) Team Coaching

1. The BIG Rules

   a. No one makes a statement, except in answer to a question.

   b. Anyone can ask anyone else a question, including the entire group.

   c. The coach can stop the proceedings to enhance learning or comment on the process.

2. Problem presenter takes only a few minutes to express the problem or issue.

   a. The problem presenter can also ask questions to clarify the problem.

   b. Team members each write down what they think the problem is and reads it out loud to check with problem presenter for agreement.

   c. After team understands the "real" problem, the coach uses the Leadership Action Learning (LAL) team coaching process to help solve the problem.

   d. Coach is in charge of the coaching process, NOT the content—the team members are content experts.

3. Team stays open to what they might "learn" about being a good leader.

   a. LAL (asking questions) slows down our thinking—avoids jumping to rapid, faulty conclusions. LAL produces deliberate, diverse, and rational thought.

   b. LAL teaches good leadership traits: listening, speaking with courtesy, being respectful—the BIG leadership traits.

Chapter 8
The Dinner

Ever since Margaret had first mentioned her mother to Leon after the Thanksgiving holiday, Leon had developed an increasing interest about her mother's Alzheimer's diagnosis. They'd discussed this on several occasions, and when he finally met Margaret and her mother, Ruth Thomas, at the restaurant, he was stunned at how in that instant Ruth reminded him of Emma when she was in her 70s.

"Margaret, I'm so sorry I'm a bit late."

"No problem, we just got here. Leon, this is my mother, Ruth."

The slim, well-dressed woman in a soft grey wool suit was seated across from Margaret. Ruth had light blond-silver hair styled in a short feathered cut and her nails were perfect. She held the menu with a kind of odd, child-like curiosity.

Margaret rose, moved toward her mother, and gently put her hand on Ruth's shoulder and said, "Mom, I want to introduce you to Leon." Ruth look startled, as if rustled from a trance.

"Oh my, Margaret," Ruth replied.

Margaret had now stooped down to be at eye level with Ruth to ensure eye contact. "Mom, are you with me?"

"Of course, Margaret," she said, now fully alert.

"Mom, this is Leon Bausch, my boss," Margaret said.

Instinctively, Leon knelt down, using the chair as support, and squared off with her eye-to-eye. "Hello, Ruth. I'm Leon," he said more loudly than Margaret had ever heard the usually soft-spoken lawyer speak.

Ruth locked on immediately. "Hello, Leon, I'm Ruth." In that instant, Ruth's voice was suddenly stronger and more intentional. For the first time in months, Margaret heard her mother's authentic voice—the one she had longed to hear for so long. It was as if a switch had gone from "pause" to "on."

Leon then rose and sat in the chair right next to Ruth. Margaret sat across from them both, wondering what just happened.

The dinner was great, mainly because Margaret got a chance to eat without being too distracted by her mother, who would ask more than a few times what the special of the day was and who regularly lost or misplaced her napkin. Because Leon was right there with her, she turned to him for help. His patience and solicitous nature amazed Margaret.

"Ruth, would you like something to drink?" Leon asked, re-translating exactly what the waiter asked.

"Drink?"

"Yes, like water, iced tea, wine?"

"Oh, Harry, you know what I drink," she said with the sweetest smile Leon could imagine as she patted him on his right hand.

Leon looked at Margaret who mouthed quietly, "Iced tea."

"OK, iced tea it is, Ruth."

In the meanwhile, Margaret had written a note on a cock-tail napkin, the words: *Harry was my Dad... her husband for 45 years.*

Leon nodded with a sympathetic wince.

"Mom, this is Leon, my boss, not Harry."

"Of course, sweetie, Leon," Ruth said patting Leon's hand and smiling again, as he returned the napkin, which had slid to the floor once more, to Ruth's lap.

Dinner was a slow-motion movie punctuated by some moments of lucid conversation by Ruth about where she had grown up and how long they'd been in the community. She'd even asked Leon questions about his business. Then without much notice, she'd slip back into a kind of foggy stupor.

The next morning at the office, Margaret went in to speak to Leon.

"I'm sorry about last night. Mom was in and out. We just changed her medication based on new research just published by the Alzheimer's Association. Seems to have made the symptoms a bit worse, at least initially. Hope it wasn't too awkward for you."

"Nonsense, I had a great time last night. Remember, I had plenty of experience with my Emma. And your mother is absolutely delightful. What an attractive woman—and such a warm smile."

"Thanks. She had a great time too. Talked about it all the way home and at breakfast today."

"Maybe we could do that again sometime?"

"Sure. Of course," she said, then smiled and headed back to her office.

Over the next several weeks, Leon, Ruth, and Margaret had dinner at least once a week, and it became clear that both Leon and Ruth enjoyed their time together. One evening after dinner, while he was helping Margaret with her coat and Ruth was sitting amused and distracted, Leon asked Margaret, "Do you think it would be possible for me to take your mother out alone sometime?"

"You mean without me?"

"Well, yes, I guess that's what I mean."

"Like on a date."

Leon blushed a bit. "I'm not sure that's how I'd characterize it, but that's sort of what I'm asking."

Now it was Margaret's turn to blush, "Sure."

"Thanks."

Chapter 9
The Vision

As J.C. walked from the parking lot to Pacific's office building, the cold January wind whipped across his face and blew his hair back like a wind sock at an airport, forcing him to pull up his coat collar.

"Ahhhh," he sighed with relief upon finally entering the building. The lobby felt warm and comforting. He made his way to the chrome elevators and pressed 8.

J.C. had arrived early at the conference room because he wanted to set up the room with flip charts and sticky notes for the day's exercises. Margaret was there early, too, and chatted with J.C.

"So, Margaret, how are you doing these days?"

"Pretty well. I'm getting to understand Leon better every day."

"Quite a guy. And, he thinks the world of you."

She blushed almost instantly.

Just then the door opened and the rest of the executive team started to arrive. After everyone was assembled around the conference room table, J.C. reviewed the rules: only statements in response to questions, process versus content, and the importance of listening deeply before asking questions.

"OK. To get us started, let me just ask everyone to report in on your agreed assignments."

Leon asked to go last.

Predictably, Jake's hand popped up first and he explained what he'd found out about the competition. There were a few consulting companies larger than Pacific, and they represented about 40 percent of the estimated market share. There were 25 firms smaller than Pacific capturing 20 percent. But only two companies—Rock-Ledge and Pacific—in the same space capturing about 15 percent combined.

"Great work, Jake. And weren't you also going to look at the marketing department as well—what it might take to expand the effort were it to become more robust, sophisticated?" Sandy asked.

Jake smacked his head, "Duh, I just got carried away with the market competition!"

The folks around the table laughed. *Jake was just being Jake* seemed to be the unspoken sentiment.

"Thanks. Clara, how about you?"

"I got some mixed results," Clara said. She'd begun to look at all the support systems of the company and while everything worked well—they were all at capacity and that any expansion or redirection would take considerable retooling. She'd have to know much more about the specific intent or direction before she could do more.

Next, Isaiah explained that he had spoken to a number of stakeholders and from them had gotten a lot of questions about strategic planning. So, he had looked at strategic planning, including definitions of mission, vision, and values. He had looked at a number of strategic planning models. He explained that a lot of people had written about the topic and there were more consultants in the strategic planning space than he could have imagined.

Then he explained that he'd looked at both vision and values. Vision was kind of the ideal state in the future—like they had talked about in their last session together with J.C. Then he spoke more deliberately about what he thought the group was trying to do. "Our strategic intent, as I see it, is to one day become the gold standard for consulting in government contracting. To be THE brand that government agencies can rely on for the kind of IT systems development consulting that will ensure our democracy and a future for our country on the world stage."

"Great work," said J.C.

The expressions on the faces of the group indicated that they, too, had all been impressed, especially Leon.

"So, Margaret, how about you, what'd you find?"

"I'm afraid not much." She explained that a couple of folks who'd been around remembered an attempt at codifying company values and mission statement, but the original owner was so entrepreneurial that it depended on which week you spoke to him about what the mission was!

"OK, thanks. Sandy, how about you?"

"Well, I pulled a quick study together to continue the SWOT analysis, but haven't had the time to pull it all into a chart. I'm sorry. In the middle of all this, we got a letter from IRS that I had to scramble to research and respond to within a short time frame."

"Well, that certainly takes priority. No sense neatly arranging the deck chairs when a tidal wave may be headed your way!"

"No, indeed, "she said with a smile.

"OK… that means we have a pretty clean slate. Leon, did you want to make some comments before we get started on the next round?"

"Actually, no. I like where this is going and would just as soon move ahead."

With that J.C. posted the now very familiar coaching diagram on the wall in plain view.

He reviewed the process—the four key questions: Who, What, How, and Open-Ended. Also the Four I's: The Issue, Impact, Ideal, and Intention.

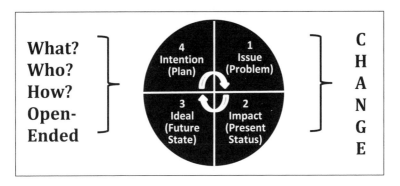

"Before we dive into the session today, do we still agree on the issue?"

There was a bit of a deer-in-the headlights look at first.

"So, can anyone articulate the issue once again?"

Margaret opened her notebook and read from it:

1. Leon has great hopes for Pacific and wants us all to come up with an ideal future vision and a path toward it—a new strategy.

2. Leon cares about the future of Pacific.

3. We need a vision, or we'll never play with the big boys.

4. The vision has something to do with clarity for clients as well as clarity for our own team.

5. How do we help others see their vision and strategy for a better future, if we don't have our own strategy?

Leon said #5 hits the closest to what he's feeling. How do we do our job for our clients—help them with consulting strategy, vision and clarity—when we can't do it for ourselves? Yes, I think that's the big issue for me."

"Impressive notes. Thanks, Margaret," J.C. said.

"OK, so let's get back into our leadership action learning team coaching mode. So, who has the first question for someone or the entire group?"

Jake's hand shot into the air.

Most of this initial session revolved around the basic question: Where do we go from here? Lots of ideas popped up from the questions and responses. The group thought that the Vision, Values, and Mission statements for the company were critical. To do that, they needed to do a complete Strengths-Weaknesses-Opportunities-Threat (SWOT) analysis with all the main stakeholders: Investors, employees, and customers.

After more probing questions, Sandy agreed to coordinate that for the next meeting. Leon also asked her, as the CFO, to work with him as he fleshed out the ESOP. She smiled and nodded yes.

Then, J.C. asked, "Are there any further questions?"

Isaiah posed questions to probe issues around strategic intent—what do we really want to get done? And, he also wanted to discuss the team's hypothesis about Pacific's future.

Jake blurted out what most others were likely thinking. "This sounds more like a science experiment than strategic planning. Can you tell me more?"

"Based on what I've read, strategic thinking really is like a science experiment," Isaiah said. He explained that a hypothesis is a way of guessing about what might happen if you do this or that. If you changed your product line, what did you think—based on context and history—the market would do? And the best way was to study the past and test the future.

"So, if I think my girlfriend likes roses, and I buy her a dozen red roses," Jake joked, "then my chances of having a good night are—well, at an advantage! Is that right?"

Isaiah smiled, "Well, I was thinking more in a corporate way, but I suppose so."

Isaiah then shifted position, cleared his throat, and said, "Jake, think of it this way," and then explained by way of example. Suppose Pacific had a lot of individual IT solutions that it had developed over time for its government clients... and then a new federal agency comes to Pacific and wants a more sophisticated enterprise-wide approach. The company's hypothesis might be that if the company could pull all our solutions together into a coherent enterprise approach, the new agency client might like it. And if that agency does like the approach, Pacific might "guess" or hypothesize that its other established agency clients might also like that same approach.

"So we try it—we experiment in our marketing with this 'new enterprise solution' and keep track of what they like and don't," Isaiah said. "Thus, we modify and perfect our approach."

"Excellent example, Isaiah," Sandy said. "Excellent."

Then, Margaret asked, "May I make a comment in response to Isaiah's example?"

J.C. looked around and said, "Sure."

"OK. So, actually," Margaret said, "Isaiah may have really hit on something in his hypothetical example." She stopped for a moment.

J.C. waited and suppressed Jake's waving hand. Then Margaret continued. "So, let's say that our strategic intent lies in being the gold standard of government IT solutions. Wouldn't it make sense for us to develop a more sophisticated, even scalable, enterprise approach to our solutions?"

"Bingo," Jake said, and everyone laughed.

"Margaret, thanks for that insight," J.C. said. "I think we have a good question to address, thanks to Margaret—Is it worth developing a scalable enterprise approach to solutions? So, who wants to comment?"

Jake's hand popped up again and everyone smiled.

The discussion went on for another half-hour, when J.C. stopped the group to consider what they might each do before the next meeting. Everyone volunteered for an assignment. Finally, Clara volunteered to write up the notes from today and get them to everyone.

With that, J.C. and the group set the next meeting date and adjourned the meeting.

Chapter 10
The Showdown

With his long-time lawyer Paul Lacey, Leon sat at the counsel table before the administrative law judge that the Government Accounting Office (GAO) had arranged to adjudicate the ongoing dispute between Rock-Ledge and Pacific Consulting. Tom Graff sat next to his attorney, an attractive young woman named Sandra O'Day. Whispering into her ear, Graff snickered like a snarky school boy.

When the Honorable Jorge Jimenez appeared, everyone stood and then all were asked to sit down. The court administrator read the complaint:

> *Pursuant to the Administrative Procedures Act of 1946 all federal executive agencies may adjudicate rules and procedures pursuant to the government's best interest as well as fairness to all parties involved. Today's proceedings deal with a claim that Rock-Ledge Consulting has launched a targeted harassment campaign against Pacific Consulting.*

The trial began. And shortly Paul Lacey was on his feet arguing Leon's case. He explained that in the last 10 government contracts, Rock-Ledge always registered its bid usually one to two weeks following the date of Pacific's bid. He showed this consistency of action in a chart he offered to the judge.

"Further, while Rock-Ledge has protested every bid it has lost to Pacific, it has protested only one other bid by another company, which coincidently is also owned by my client, Leon Bausch. These apparently vindictive and targeted lawsuits...."

"Objection, your honor, Counsel is attempting to characterize my client without having substantiated a sufficient basis for his scurrilous attack," O'Day said.

The two lawyers went back and forth. But eventually the judge brought them back to the case at hand. About 15 minutes later, Paul finished and asked for a speedy adjudication because these frivolous filings were wasting time and costing Leon Bausch a lot of money.

Graff's attorney argued that both businesses competed in identical areas—information security and cloud computing—the two hottest areas in the federal government contracting space. Of course, they would butt heads, she resolved. "Fair competition is what makes this country's economic system work. And now Mr. Bausch would like to halt the American marketplace. It makes no sense, your Honor."

After much debate, discord, diversion, and a lunch break, all parties once again sat in front of the judge. A large man with a deeply resonant voice, Judge Jimenez leaned forward and looked at Tom and then at Leon. "Gentlemen, I have read both affidavits and reviewed the history, and listened to your arguments."

He paused to sip water. "I also read a report by a friend of the court—what we call *amicus curiae*—who is an expert on such matters, Mr. John Fraserly. Mr. Fraserly is the CEO of a prominent government contracting firm. He's a documented expert who has founded and sold two large government contracting firms and who has taught government contracting at George Washington University.

"I have his report before me, and I have had two other experts—both prominent contracting lawyers in the field— review the matter before this court. All three agree on one thing, as do I after reading their reports and listening to your arguments. Mr. Graff, in the opinion of this court, your actions have been both frivolous and vindictive."

Tom Graff's face turned beet red. He glared at the judge who stared back at him until Graff looked away.

"This court, therefore, rules in favor of the plaintiff, Mr. Bausch and Pacific Consulting."

Leon simply nodded his head once.

The judge continued, "Based on the review conducted by my advisors, a number of serious improprieties were discovered, including violation of a non-disclosure agreement between Mr. Graff and Mr. Bausch as well as a more serious issue of potential egregious theft of intellectual property on the part of Mr. Graff. The court suggests that Mr. Bausch consider seeking damages from Rock-Ledge and Mr. Graff personally and notes that I would be happy to refer this matter to federal court."

Tom Graff was scribbling notes and stabbing his finger at the page for his attorney to look at. And she shook her head "No"... several times... all the while trying to keep her attention on the judge.

"Counsel, do you or Mr. Graff wish to address the court?" the judge asked.

"No, your Honor," O'Day said, glaring at her client. "No, we do not. Thank you, your Honor.

"Very well," the judge said, turning to Paul Lacey. "Mr. Lacey, do you or your client wish to address the court?"

He looked at Leon who shook his head sideways softly and slowly.

"No thank you, your Honor," Paul Lacey replied.

The judge nodded and then spoke, "Then I have a couple of things to say. First, Mr. Bausch, this court apologizes for the federal contracting bid-protest system that has put you through the wringer. Second, Mr. Graff, this court warns you as sternly as it can to cease and desist targeting any entity that Mr. Bausch owns, operates, or for that matter walks by, as far as I'm concerned. Not only are you close to severe financial sanctions, but also you may be dangerously close to federal civil issues as well. You are officially put on notice," the judge said, striking his gavel. "This court is adjourned."

When Leon came into the office the next morning, the office was decorated with streamers and everyone greeted him with a huge round of applause. At first, Leon thought it was a birthday party for someone in the office but quickly realized that it was a celebration for him. He was embarrassed and simply waved and mouthed, "Thank you."

After a bit of nodding and smiling, he went into his office, closed the door, flopped into his chair, and called the doctor.

Chapter 11
The Progression

When he was much younger, Leon, like so many, had played the game "What would you do if you had only six months to live?" In fact, he'd gone so far as to write it down and put it in a frame on his desk. And to keep it top of mind, he moved the frame around every week for the past 50 years since he'd created the list. Surprisingly, the words never had to be changed.

And when he arrived at his office the day after his court victory and sat down, he pulled the now-faded wooden frame to him and read it under his breath:

> With six months to live, I'd like to be known as the following when I died:
>
> 1. A good businessman.
>
> 2. A devoted husband and father.
>
> 3. A philanthropist.

He quietly nodded his head. He'd been a successful and ethical businessman, by anyone's account. He'd bought and sold several companies, each of which prospered, as did its employees, along with the community. Leon had been a quiet and powerful voice in the business community—served on boards, helped many young business leaders get their start, and voiced his opinion whenever he saw things that violated good business or ethics. He'd been called a man of courage when he left the company he'd worked at before Pacific.

Leon paused when he read the second line, "a devoted husband and father." His eyes brimmed with tears, which he held back by dabbing each eye with his fingers. He thought of Emma's illness and how he'd fought back every day as his caretaking increased while she slipped beneath the waters of rationality like someone drowning and just out of his grasp. He thought of her pregnancies and the hope they both brought. Then, the two miscarriages and the despair they brought, especially the last one—their last hope before the emergency hysterectomy. They would have had a daughter had there been no miscarriage. He dabbed his eyes now, but the dams in his eyes gave way to the torrent behind them, and he wept alone at his big desk. When he'd stopped crying, Leon thought of Margaret and her mother, Ruth. Ruth reminded him so much of Emma, and Margaret, in that very instant, reminded him of the daughter he had never had. It felt natural, this progression of their relationship.

Finally, he looked at the last line. "A philanthropist." Leon thought of the many nonprofits he'd worked for, starting with Big Brothers when he was in college. He'd been on more nonprofit boards than anyone in the town and had been given so many awards that he'd been too embarrassed to display them, so he'd stored them in a pile of boxes in his basement. Life had been good to him, and he had always thought it made sense to do what his mother had taught him—to give back to others. So, he did.

Just then, Leon heard a soft knock on the door. He knew that knock well. "Come in, Margaret." She was beaming today, even more than usual.

"How are you today?" he asked with more purpose than usual.

"Just great, thanks!"

"You seem even more happy than usual."

She paused, "Thanks, I am."

"Would I be intruding if I asked why?"

"Well, my mother has just been accepted for an Alzheimer's experimental drug program—a clinical trial on a super new drug. I'm just praying she's in the segment that gets the drug, not the placebo."

"Congratulations," Leon said, recalling the same elation he had when Emma got into a similar study that like many Alzheimer medications had proved to be a blind alley. "Maybe we should celebrate at dinner tonight?"

"That would be great!" she said as she smiled, picked up two signed contracts from his desk, and started toward the door.

Then Leon got a bit more serious. "Margaret, can you stay for just a few minutes more. I'd like to talk to you." He pointed toward the chair next to his desk—the one he reserved for important guests.

"Sure," she said and then sat down feeling a bit like an imposter sitting in this particular chair.

Leon began, "This morning I met with my doctor."

"I see," she said softly.

Leon cleared his throat, "Look, you no doubt wonder why I drag my right leg. Most people assume I've had a stroke, but are polite enough not to ask."

He hesitated and then said, "I have small tumor—about the size of a pea—on the front of my brain, a place they call the prefrontal cortex. It's the part of the brain that among other things keeps emotions in check and edits what you say—like an editor who screens what you're writing before you actually publish it."

At first Margaret just stared. "Oh my! Mr. Bausch! I'm so...so sorry," she then said, and put her hand to her mouth. Tears welled up, clouding up her clear blue eyes.

Leon went on to explain that the doctors weren't sure how bad it was. Eventually, he'd have to have it operated on, but Leon had been optimistic based on the small size and the location in the brain. However, he'd discovered that something was wrong just before he bought Pacific. He had in fact had a mini-stroke, which was the reason his right foot dragged. The treatment he got immediately after the stroke saved his life.

"I'm telling you all of this confidentially, because you'll quite literally become my 'right-hand' and my 'right brain' as we go forward. I'll tell the staff when the timing is right. Can you do that for me, keep a confidence and help me manage through this?"

"Of course, Mr. Bausch."

"Thank you, Margaret, I appreciate that very much."

"You're welcome," she said. She stood, thinking she was dismissed.

He motioned her to sit down. "I want to ask you one more favor. And I promise you that it's the last one—at least for today," he said, a smile lighting up his face. "I'm going to suggest that you attend the Executive MBA at the University of Virginia's Darden Business School."

"MBA... Darden...I...I'm not sure I'm capable. I, I certainly don't have the money. I..."

"I've already done the homework," Leon said, "J.C. has made some inquiries and feels confident you'd get in. You do recall he taught there for years."

She nodded.

He continued, "And of course, we'd give you all the time you needed for coursework and study and pay for all the costs."

"Mr. Bausch... I'm, I mean, I don't know what to say."

"So, just say yes!"

"OK...yes."

Chapter 12
The Changes

Following his meeting with Margaret, Leon asked Isaiah to step into his office when he had a chance. About 20 minutes later, the tall, lean COO presented himself at Leon's door and was beckoned in. Leon pulled out the chair for him—again the one next to his desk for special guests. Isaiah nodded his thanks along with registering a brief eyebrow twitch, about as much as he got excited and showed it to anyone.

Leon began, "How many years have we known each other now?"

Isaiah searched his memory, he said, "Counting my part time work with you in graduate school, twelve years."

"Time does fly! My goodness, twelve years. We've been through a lot together in more than a decade, haven't we?"

"Y-e-s," Isaiah said dragging out his answer, as if to say: *Hey, what's this all about?*

Leon read him well. "In that time, have you ever known me to make a reckless decision?"

"No, Leon. Hey, is this about something I did or didn't do? I feel like I'm being cross-examined in court."

Leon felt a flush of guilt for acting like a lawyer. "I apologize. I can see how you'd feel that way. It's just that I have something weighing heavily on my mind," he said pausing. Then he continued in a slower, more deliberate tone. "I've had a dormant brain tumor for several years. It's the reason I limp. And this morning, my doctor told me it had started to grow. It will eventually require surgery."

Those words hit Isaiah in the gut like a fist in a boxing match. "What....Leon....God....I'm so, so sorry."

"I'm sorry to start off your day with all this stuff. But I wanted to let you know before the rest of the team... that is, besides Margaret, who also knows. The reason I told her was to prepare her to act as my brain's filter. Based on the tumor's location, I might be prone, so the doctor says, to make more rash judgments, ones that could affect the company."

"I see... like a brain referee?"

Leon smiled, "I guess you could call it that."

"I'm also going to appoint you as president."

"Leon, there's no need for that."

"There most certainly is."

Leon explained that removing himself from the daily operations by having Isaiah as president gave the company a second and an official firewall. Leon did not want to do anything that would ever hurt the company or its employees. And while he wasn't certain about the timing of his surgery, he never wanted it to have a negative impact on the company.

"So you'll be the company's first line of defense and Margaret the second. Does that make sense?"

"Yes, but I feel awkward."

"Don't worry. It makes me feel good to have you at the helm, especially given the uncertainties ahead for me."

Leon stuck out his right hand. As the two men shook hands, Leon drew his left hand over to seal the handshake with a fatherly pat on the back of Leon's hand.

Leon then called Margaret back in to join them. He moved the conversation to a seating area nearer the back of his office. "OK, so where do we want to start regarding the transition that will start today?" he asked Leon and Margaret.

About two hours later, with still many questions bubbling, especially in Margaret's head, Leon said, "I think I want to tell the rest of the crew. I'm calling a meeting for 3 p.m., and I've asked J.C. to join us as well."

Isaiah looked at Margaret and both of them smiled, knowing that Leon had already played this scenario out in his head and had it timed down to the hour!

It was not odd for Leon to hold staff meetings, but usually he gave plenty of notice, they were never on Friday afternoons or Monday mornings, and J.C. usually only attended the action learning team meetings.

Everyone was seated when Leon came in, this time using a cane. A couple of them darted looks back and forth at each other. With some effort, he sat down at the head of the table.

"Thank you all for coming on short notice and on a late Friday afternoon. I promise to get you home to your families on time and in one piece!"

Everyone smiled, cautiously.

"I have some important announcements that will be made by e-mail, directly following this meeting."

He explained the tumor.

Everyone, including Isaiah and Margaret, looked saddened after Leon made the announcement about his health situation. Hearing it a second time did not seem to soften the blow.

Jake, the bellwether of the group, said, "Oh my God, Leon, I feel awful for you!"

Leon nodded as if taking a compliment.

Clara dabbed her eyes. Sandy just stared, transfixed.

"I'm telling you all this in preparation for us moving forward strategically as a team. So, here's the plan: First, I've asked J.C. to continue to coach us through our strategic plan—one that gives us a clear path past obstacles and barriers and helps us reach our dreams."

Judging by the nods in J.C.'s direction, it appeared that everyone liked that idea a lot.

"OK. Next I'm announcing that Isaiah become the new president of Pacific as of Monday."

The team members stared at Leon, then at Isaiah, who briefly bowed his head, embarrassed by the news and the attention.

"Most of you know that Isaiah and I have known each other for over a decade. I trust no one more than him."

Leon then explained Margaret's role and his need for two layers of protection for the organization: Isaiah and Margaret.

"But, Leon, aren't you moving a little fast?" Sandy said. "Look, I have every confidence in Isaiah and Margaret. And you know you can rely on every one of us in this room. But restructuring before you know the extent..." she stopped short and terminated her sentence.

"Sandy, I've known about this for some time. It's just gotten more pronounced. Just think of this as succession planning in action," he said, smiling as she dabbed her eyes with a tissue and nodded.

Chapter 13
The Plan

Over the next six months a lot happened. Leon had the operation to have the tumor removed. It was about the size of a grape, the doctor said, and had begun affecting Leon's decision making and balance. Following the operation, his speech was definitely impaired, and he needed months of occupational, speech, and physical therapy. And while he had a nurse with him full time, Margaret was almost constantly back and forth between the company and the hospital and later his home—especially at critical times. When Leon began to regain his faculties, she read to him minutes from meetings, told him about what was going on in the company, and wrote out his messages to various folks. She was his eyes and ears, hands and feet.

As Leon's recovery progressed, he asked Margaret if she could bring her mother around for visits. Ruth began to visit Leon with Margaret every Sunday. By then, Leon was sitting in a chair comfortably and could walk with the assistance of a walker. But whenever they came together, Leon had spent hours with the nurse, getting ready, dressed, shaved, and seated in his big leather wing chair before their arrival. It was as if Sunday became his weekly goal. And every week, Leon seemed more confident and happy, as were his friends and caregivers.

Indeed, the doctors had been not only pleased at the results, but also astonished with his recovery, given the operation and his age. Of course, Leon attributed his recovery to his doctors, nurses, Margaret, and the company—everyone other than himself. But everyone, including his great executive team, knew that at the center of his climb back was the indomitable spirit of Leon Bausch.

The team had pulled together a plan to make Pacific a "resonant company" that was in tune with its clients, employees, and investors. In fact, being "in tune" became the company's mantra. So, if something began to veer off track, someone on the executive team might say, "I'm sensing that we're not in tune today," and everyone would get the picture quickly.

The plan identified two areas of growth for the company: information security and cloud computing consulting. As a result, Isaiah decided to invest heavily in education and training of their people in this area. Recruitment focused its efforts on hiring people with both the right background and the right cultural fit for Pacific. Technology got aligned. The company invested in hardware and software focused on these two important areas. New business models and processes were put in place to meet the needs of not only government but also the private sector. Isaiah had thought that a more diversified portfolio—both government and private sector—would secure the company's future. J.C. had been amazed at Isaiah's insights and admired him more each time the team met.

In August, Margaret started at Darden. Her class contained mostly men, with about 10 women—all of whom she liked. The women had bonded quickly, and she had already learned so much at times she thought her head would burst. The case studies, the simulations, the study groups—everything excited her and opened up her mind. It was if she were learning things that she could use Monday morning at the office. And Leon loved what he was seeing—this amazing young woman developing into a real leader, week by week.

Isaiah was settling into his role as the future CEO. Leon had sent him to both Wharton and Harvard for courses on executive leadership and strategy. The one- and two-week courses fit his learning style. Besides, he was able to take his bike with him. An avid cyclist, Isaiah had taken these work sabbaticals as a chance to train really hard in different parts of the country. He'd fallen in love with Cambridge and met some cool folks to cycle with at Wharton. Life was good, and Leon had noticed how more open he was to options and long-term discussions.

Sandy had become a mentor to Clara, who was developing as a real leader in the company. The two of them started to socialize after work and had even taken a couple of weekends together at the beach that summer.

And Jake, well, was Jake. He continued to be a catalyst at meetings but had also learned to listen more. Leon had taken on the job of mentoring him at work—a job that had brought both Jake and him tremendous satisfaction.

The "plan" had started to come together, Leon thought. Pacific began maturing because the employees had decided to move toward new, hard goals as a team. Everyone began to see the other's strengths and play off them. And clients started to pick up the company's strong leadership "Wi-Fi" signals, as Leon called it.

As he explained at one of his last executive meetings with the team, "Great leaders give off a signal to people around them. It's like Wi-Fi. Actually, the science is that we all have mirror neurons that pick up other people's emotional Wi-Fi. And leaders are super transmitters. People sense their powerful signals and adapt quickly."

He explained that because of that, when you get a whole team of leaders in sync, the power of the signal is so potent that clients, employees, investors, and even competitors pick up that something's happening and defer to it. Great leadership is truly resonating with the environment.

"You guys are really resonating these days, and it makes me proud," he said, smiling as broadly as his face allowed.

As the months rolled by and he began to walk and get stronger, Leon had been spending more and more time with Ruth. The two had become companions, enjoying quiet dinners together, longer and longer walks, and often just sitting together. During their time together Leon began to notice that as he got stronger, Ruth's cognitive capacity had waned. She was forgetting more frequently. Her short-term memory was almost completely depleted. In fact, she'd been calling him "Harry," her dead husband's name, almost all the time now. Leon didn't mind it a bit. In fact, he was honored by it.

One afternoon, Leon told Margaret that he wanted to take care of Ruth's care as her condition worsened. "Absolutely not," Margaret said when he told her of his intentions. "I can afford to handle her care myself, thanks to your generosity."

"But, she's a lot like Emma to me... I insist."

"We'll talk, but I'm not keen on this idea. You've already done so much for me and our family."

"Margaret, you are family to me."

Chapter 14
The Epilogue

In the next couple of years, Pacific experienced big changes.

Within a year after his surgery, Leon began to slow down considerably and took on the title of Chairman of the company. He also joined Ruth in the same assisted living facility, in an apartment right across the hall from her. The two of them shared all their meals together and were inseparable.

Isaiah became the CEO and was feeling comfortable in his new role, though he missed the daily interaction with and wise counsel of Leon, whom he met every week for coffee. And before ascending to CEO, he appointed Sandy as the president—who had fully embraced her new, more operational role. Fortunately, Sandy had groomed Clara for the CFO position, so transition was smooth, almost effortless.

Jake continued to develop as director of marketing and sales and became active in the Chamber of Commerce and several other key community organizations. He'd begun to blossom under Isaiah's leadership and stability and in the past year sales had skyrocketed.

J.C. introduced another coach, Maria Lisbon, to Isaiah to take over for him. J.C. had become fond of Margaret and ethically did not want to confuse his coaching of the team with his feelings for her. After he had resigned as team coach, he and Margaret had begun to date.

Margaret graduated from Darden at the top of her class. In fact, she was selected as class spokesperson at the final dinner in the Rotunda at UVa. J.C. was there with his former academic colleagues—feeling as if he'd never left. However, despite their cajoling him to come back home to academia, J.C. resisted in favor of what he called "*working in the real world of leadership.*"

Finally, at Christmas, J.C. proposed to Margaret, only after he had talked to Leon and Ruth—who smiled pleasantly and still called Leon, Harry.

Offerings by Steve Gladis

Motivational Speaking

Steve Gladis provides an inspiring, engaging, and energizing session. Engagement venues can include the following:

- Company meetings
- Breakfast, lunch, or dinner keynotes
- Leadership retreats

"Terrific speaker... entertaining and informative style. Time flew and I learned a lot."

– Bank of America participant

Special Note: Engage Steve Gladis as a speaker and receive special book discounts for orders of more than 100 copies and a speech and book signing by the author.

Leadership Training and Development

- Workshop sessions tailored to meet the specific needs of your organization

- Workshop length can vary based on session objectives and agenda

"Excellent course; very dynamic instructor. I took away many new insights as well as practical tips."

– U.S. Government Accountability Office Participant

Executive Coaching

Steve Gladis has coached many executives in both the corporate and public service/government sectors:

- CEOs
- C-level executives
- Executive teams

Other Books by Steve Gladis

The Agile Leader (HRD Press, 2011)

A leadership fable, *The Agile Leader* is the story of a leader, Luke Hopkins, who leads a national sales team. As he starts making changes and drives his team to achieve corporate sales goals, he runs right into the conflict, resistive culture, and company politics that all leaders must navigate to be successful. A former standout college quarterback, Luke seeks out his old football coach, Coach Danforth (Coach D) only to find out that he's died. However, his daughter Allison was given the Coach's last "Playbook for Leaders." She and Luke strike up a strong friendship, and using the tenets Coach D. wrote about (and illustrated with diagrams), Luke learns timely lessons from the Coach's Playbook to navigate the complex world of a corporate America. Any new or experienced leader reading this book will clearly recognize all the challenges that Luke faces as he tries to make a difference.

The Trusted Leader (HRD Press, 2010)

A leadership fable, *The Trusted Leader* is the story of a new young leader, Carlos Lopez, who gets promoted to supervise his peers. He gets conflicting advice from his boss about how to take charge, and it backfires. Confused, Carlos seeks out the best leader he's ever known, Coach Jack Dempsey. The two agree to meet regularly to talk about leadership at a local restaurant. The coach teaches Carlos about how to lead, while Carlos and the coach learn about each other's secret, sad, but ultimately formative pasts. Finally, the coach teaches Carlos about the Trust Triangle—the critical key to leadership.

The Transparent Leader (HRD Press, 2009)

Written as a business leadership fable, *The Transparent Leader* is the story of a smart emerging leader, Stephanie Marcus, as she navigates the challenging world of business.

Fortunately, she meets Lou Donaldson, who acts as a friend, informal coach, and mentor as he guides Steph through the complicated business ecosystem in which she finds herself. Throughout the story, Steph learns about clear leadership communication. She adapts and changes and becomes a more transparent—clear and open—leader. At the same time, she learns Lou's personal story, which helps her fully appreciate his wisdom. An especially good read for women in leadership positions.

The Executive Coach in the Corporate Forest (HRD Press, 2008) Foreword by Marshall Goldsmith, the world's leading executive coach

A business fable, *The Executive Coach in the Corporate Forest* is the story of a young, gifted executive coach, J. C. Williams, and his coaching relationships with his rather varied and interesting business clients—all with their own challenges. The book offers some engaging stories, has believable characters with realistic problems, and illustrates the structure and content of the coaching process. The book is a quick read and was written to explain the coaching process to executives.

The Journey of the Accidental Leader (HRD Press, 2008)

Written as a business fable, *The Journey of the Accidental Leader* is the story of a young man who, like so many people, gets thrust into a leadership position he neither wanted nor asked for. What he does and how he reacts makes the book both entertaining and informative. This book is based on the author's practical leadership experience as a Marine Corps officer in Vietnam.

Survival Writing for Business (HRD Press, 2005)

To write well, you need to keep it clear and concise. This book shows how and is a no-nonsense, virtual lifeline to writing success.

The Manager's Pocket Guide to Public Presentations
(HRD Press, 1999)

This book is an indispensable reference for managers and executives who find themselves in the unfamiliar and often frightening position of having to give a public presentation. It is a compendium of tips that will help any manager learn the survival tactics of public speaking. A simple, quick read, based on the accepted theory and practice of rhetoric, it is also a confidence builder that will help any manager begin to overcome anxiety over public speaking.

The Manager's Pocket Guide to Effective Writing
(HRD Press, 1999)

Written communication is prevalent at most levels of business, but especially at the managerial level. Your writing may be grammatically and logically sound, but is it effective? Is it conveying your message with the concision and accuracy that makes you an effective communicator? Whether you're a manager in charge of a group of writers, or just a person interested in improving his or her writing skills, *The Manager's Pocket Guide to Effective Writing* uses easy, practical, how-to steps to help you write better and ultimately make a better impression on others.

WriteType: Personality Types and Writing Styles
(HRD Press, 1994)

Based on individual personality styles, this book provides new strategies for the four basic types of writers: the correspondent, the technical writer, the creative writer, and the analytical writer. Each person fits one of these well-defined writing "types." Once readers learn their writing personality and follow the writing process suggested in the book, they find writing easier and less anxiety producing.

Contact Information:

E-mail: sgladis@stevegladis.com

Telephone: 703-424-3780

Location: The George Mason Enterprise Center
4031 University Drive, Suite 200
Fairfax, VA 22030

Visit his website: www.stevegladisleadership.com

Leadership Blog: Survival Leadership http://
survivalleadership.blogspot.com

About the Author

Steve Gladis, Ph.D.

Steve Gladis serves as president and CEO of Steve Gladis Leadership Partners, a leadership development firm focused on helping leaders and their teams achieve both success and significance through executive coaching, leadership development, and motivational speaking. Clients include executives and teams from publicly traded and private corporations, U.S. government agencies, associations, and nonprofits. At George Mason University, he teaches leadership and communication courses. The author of 17 books on leadership and communication, Steve is a former member of the University of Virginia's faculty and served as an Associate Dean and the Director of the University's Northern Virginia Center. He is currently an executive coach, certified by the International Coach Federation, for the Darden Business School's Executive MBA program and also teaches courses in leadership coaching. A former FBI special agent and decorated U.S. Marine Corps officer, he is a committed civic and academic leader. Steve serves on the Executive Boards of both the Fairfax County Chamber of Commerce and The Community Foundation of Northern Virginia and is active in philanthropic activities in the Greater Metropolitan Washington, DC area. His company donates a significant portion of its annual net profits back to the community.

Contact information:

E-mail: sgladis@stevegladis.com
Telephone: 703-424-3780
Location: The George Mason Enterprise Center
4031 University Drive, Fairfax, VA 22030